YOUR FO

 N

TO USE THEM

by

CHRISTIAN D. LARSON

COMPASS CIRCLE

Your Forces And How To Use Them.
Current edition published by Compass Circle in 2021.

Published by Compass Circle
Cover copyright ©2021 by Compass Circle.

Note:
All efforts have been made to preserve original spellings and punctuation of the original edition which may include old-fashioned English spellings of words and archaic variants.

This book is a product of its time and does not reflect the same views on race, gender, sexuality, ethnicity, and interpersonal relations as it would if it were written today.

For information contact :
information@compass-circle.com

Believe in yourself and all that you are. Know that there is something inside you that is greater than any obstacle.

CHRISTIAN D. LARSON

SECRET WISDOM OF THE AGES SERIES

Life presents itself, it advances in a fast way. Life indeed never stops. It never stops until the end. The most diverse questions peek and fade in our minds. Sometimes we seek for answers. Sometimes we just let time go by.

The book you have now in your hands has been waiting to be discovered by you. This book may reveal the answers to some of your questions.

Books are friends. Friends who are always by your side and who can give you great ideas, advice or just comfort your soul.

A great book can make you see things in your soul that you have not yet discovered, make you see things in your soul that you were not aware of.

Great books can change your life for the better. They can make you understand fascinating theories, give you new ideas, inspire you to undertake new challenges or to walk along new paths.

Life philosophies like the one of Christian D. Larson are indeed a secret to many, but for those of us lucky enough to have discovered them, by one way or another, these books can enlighten us. They can open a wide range of possibilities to us. Because achieving greatness requires knowledge.

The series SECRET WISDOM OF THE AGES presented by Compass Circle try to bring you the great timeless masterpieces of personal development, positive thinking, and the law of attraction.

We welcome you to discover with us fascinating works by Neville Goddard, Joseph Murphy, Wallace Wattles, Thomas Troward, James Allen, among others.

Contents

FOREWORD

"THERE are a million energies in man. What may we not become when we learn to use them all." This is the declaration of the poet; and though poetry is usually inspired by transcendental visions, and therefore more or less impressed with apparent exaggerations, nevertheless there is in this poetic expression far more actual, practical truth than we may at first believe.

How many energies there are in man, no one knows; but there are so many that even the keenest observers of human activity have found it impossible to count them all. And as most of these energies are remarkable, to say the least, and some of them so remarkable as to appear both limitless in power and numberless in possibilities, we may well wonder what man will become when he learns to use them all.

When we look upon human nature in general we may fail to see much improvement in power and worth as compared with what we believe the race has been in the past; and therefore we conclude that humanity will continue to remain about the same upon this planet until the end of time. But when we investigate the lives of such individuals as have recently tried to apply more intelligently the greater powers within them, we come to a different conclusion. We then discover that there is evidence in thousands of human lives of a new and superior race of people—a race that will apply a much larger measure of the wonders and possibilities that exist within them.

It is only a few years, not more than a quarter of a century, since modern psychology began to proclaim the new science of human thought and action, so that we have had but a short time to demonstrate what a more intelligent application of our energies and forces can accomplish. But already the evidence is coming in from all sources, revealing results that frequently border upon the extraordinary. Man can do far more with himself and his life than he has been doing in the past; he can call into action, and successfully apply, far more ability, energy and worth than his forefathers ever dreamed of. So much has been proven during this brief introductory period of the new-age. Then. what greater things may we not reasonably expect when we have had fifty or a hundred years more in which to develop and apply those larger possibilities which we now know to be inherent in us all.

It is the purpose of the following pages, not only to discuss these greater powers and possibilities in man, but also to present practical methods through which they may be applied. We have been aware of the fact for centuries that there is more in man than what appears on the surface, but it is only in recent years that a systematic effort has been made to understand the nature and practical use of this "more," as well as to work out better methods for the thorough and effective application of those things on the surface which we have always employed. In dealing with a subject that is so large and so new, however, it is necessary to make many statements that may, at first sight, appear to be unfounded, or at least exaggerations. But if the reader will thoroughly investigate the basis of such statements as he goes along, he will not only find that there are no unfounded statements or exaggerations in the book, but will wish that every strong statement made had been made many times as strong.

When we go beneath the surface of human life and learn what greater things are hidden beneath the ordinary layers of mental substance and vital energy, we find man to be so wonderfully made that language is wholly inadequate to

1

describe even a fraction of his larger and richer life. We may try to give expression to our thoughts, at such times, by employing the strongest statements and the most forceful adjectives that we can think of; but even these prove little better than nothing; so therefore we may conclude that no statement that attempts to describe the "more" in man can possibly be too strong. Even the strongest fails to say one thousandth of what we would say should we speak the whole truth. We shall all admit this, and accordingly shall find it advisable not to pass judgement upon strong statements but to learn to understand and apply those greater powers within ourselves that are infinitely stronger than the strongest statement that could possibly be made.

Those minds who may believe that the human race is to continue weak and imperfect as usual, should consider what remarkable steps in advance have recently been taken in nearly all fields of human activity. And then they should remember that the greater powers in man, as well as a scientific study of the use of his lesser powers, have been almost wholly neglected. The question then that will naturally arise is, what man might make of himself if he would apply the same painstaking science to his own development and advancement as he now applies in other fields. If he did, would we not, in another generation or two, witness unmistakable evidence of the coming of a new and superior race, and would not strong men and women become far more numerous than ever before in the history of the world?

Each individual will want to answer these questions according to his own point of view, but whatever his answer may be, we all must agree that man can be, become and achieve far more than even the most sanguine indications of the present may predict. And it is the purpose of the following pages to encourage as many people as possible to study and apply these greater powers within them so that they may not only become greater and richer and more worthy as individuals, but may also become the forerunners of that higher and more wonderful race of which we all have so fondly dreamed.

PROMISE YOURSELF

To be so strong that nothing can disturb your peace of mind.

To talk health, happiness and prosperity to every person you meet.

To make all your friends feel that there is something in them.

To look at the sunny side of everything and make your optimism come true.

To think only of the best, to work only for the best, and to expect only the best.

To be just as enthusiastic about the success of others as you are about your own.

To forget the mistakes of the past and press on to the greater achievements of the future.

To wear a cheerful countenance at all timed and give every living creature you meet a smile.

To give so much time to the improvement of yourself that you have no time to criticise others.

To be too large for worry, too noble for anger, too strong for fear; and too happy to permit the presence of trouble.

To think well of yourself and to proclaim this fact to the world, not in loud words but in great deeds.

To live in the faith that the whole world is on your side so long as you are true to the best that is in you.

Passage of a Soul

YOUR FORCES AND HOW TO USE THEM

THE RULING PRINCIPLES OF MAN

THE purpose of the following pages will be to work out the subject chosen in the most thorough and practical manner; in brief, to analyse the whole nature of man, find all the forces in his possession, whether they be apparent or hidden, active or dormant, and to present methods through which all those forces can be applied in making the life of each individual richer, greater and better. To make every phase of this work as useful as possible to the greatest number possible, not a single statement will be made that all cannot understand, and not a single idea will be presented that anyone cannot apply to everyday life.

We all want to know what we actually possess both in the physical, the mental and the spiritual, and we want to know how the elements and forces within us can be applied in the most successful manner. It is results in practical life that we want, and we are not true to ourselves or the race until we learn to use the powers within us so effectively, that the greatest results possible within the possibilities of human nature are secured.

When we proceed with a scientific study of the subject, we find that the problem before us is to know what is in us and how to use what is in us. After much study of the powers in man, both conscious and subconscious, we have come to the conclusion that if we only knew how to use these powers, we could accomplish practically anything that we may have in view, and not only realize our wants to the fullest degree, but also reach even our highest goal. Though this may seem to be a strong statement, nevertheless when we examine the whole nature of man, we are compelled to admit that it is true even in its fullest sense, and that therefore, not a single individual can fail to realize his wants and reach his goal, after he has learned how to use the powers that are in him.This is not mere speculation, nor is it simply a beautiful dream. The more we study the lives of people who have achieved, and the more we study our own experience every day, the more convinced we become that there is no reason whatever why any individual should not realize all his ambitions and much more.

The basis of this study will naturally be found in the understanding of the whole nature of man, as we must know what we are, before we can know and use what we in inherently possess. In analysing human nature a number of methods have been employed, but there are only three in particular that are of actual value for our present purpose. The first of these declares that man is composed of ego, consciousness and form, and though this analysis is the most complete, yet it is also the most abstract, and is therefore not easily understood. The second analysis, which is simpler, and which is employed almost exclusively by the majority, declares that man is body, mind and soul; but as much as this idea is thought of and spoken of there are very few who actually understand it. In fact, the usual conception of man as body, mind and soul will have to be completely reversed in order to become absolutely true. The third analysis, which is the simplest and the most serviceable, declares that man is composed of individuality and personality, and it is this conception of human nature that will constitute the phases of our study in this work.

Before we pass to the more practical side of the subject, we shall find it profitable to examine briefly these various ideas concerning the nature of man; in fact, every part of our human analysis that refers to the ego, simply must be understood if we are to learn how to use the forces we possess, and the reason for this is found in the fact that the ego is the "I Am," the ruling principle in man, the centre and source of individuality, the originator of everything that takes place in man, and that primary something to which all other things in human nature are secondary.

When the average person employs the term "ego," he thinks that he is dealing with something that is hidden so deeply in the abstract that it can make but little difference whether we understand it or not. This, however, does not happen to be true, because it is the ego that must act before any action can take place anywhere in the human system, and it is the ego that must originate the new before any step in advance can be taken. And in addition, it is extremely important to realize that the power of will to control the forces we possess, depends directly upon how fully conscious we are of the ego as the ruling principle within us. We understand therefore, that it is absolutely necessary to associate all thought, all, feeling and all actions of mind or personality with the ego, or what we shall hereafter speak of as the "I Am."

The first step to be taken in this connection, is to recognize the "I Am" in everything you do, and to think always of the "I Am," as being you—the supreme you. Whenever you think, realize that it is the "I Am" that originated the thought. Whenever you act, realize that it is the "I Am" that gives initiative to that action, and whenever you think of yourself or try to be conscious of yourself, realize that the "I Am" occupies the throne of your entire field of consciousness.

Another important essential is to affirm silently in your own mind that you are the "I AM," and as you affirm this statement or as you simply declare positively, "I Am" think of the "I Am" as being the ruling principle in your whole world, as being distinct and above and superior to all else in your being, and as being you, yourself, in the highest, largest, and most comprehensive sense. You thus lift yourself up, so to speak, to the mountain top of masterful individuality; you enthrone yourself; you become true to yourself; you place yourself where you belong.

Through this practice you not only discover yourself to be the master of your whole life, but you elevate all your conscious actions to that lofty state in your consciousness that we may describe as the throne of your being, or as that centre of action within which the ruling "I Am" lives and moves and has its being. If you wish to control and direct the forces you possess, you must act from the throne of your being, so to speak or in other words, from that conscious point in your mental world wherein all power of control, direction and initiative proceeds; and this point of action is the centre of the "I Am." You must act, not as a body, not as a personality, not as a, mind, but as the "I Am," and the more fully you recognize the lofty position of the "I Am," the greater becomes your power to control and direct all other things that you may possess. In brief, whenever you think or act, you should feel that you stand with the "I Am," at the apex of mentality on the very heights of your existence, and you should at the same time, realize that this "I Am" is you—the supreme you. The more you practice these methods, the more you lift yourself up above the limitations of mind and body, into the realization of your own true position as a masterful individuality; in fact, you place yourself where you belong, over and above everything in your organised existence.

When we examine the mind of the average person, we find that they usually identify themselves with mind or body. They either think that they are body or that they are mind, and therefore they can control neither mind nor body. The "I Am" in their nature is submerged in a bundle of ideas, some of which are true and some of which are not, and their thought is usually controlled by those ideas without receiving any direction whatever from that principle within them that alone was intended to give direction. Such a one lives in the lower story of human existence but as we can control life only when we give directions from the upper story, we discover just why the average person neither understands their forces nor has the power to use them. They must first elevate themselves to the upper story of the human structure, and the first and most important step to be taken in this direction is to recognize the "I AM" as the ruling principle and that the "I Am" is you.

Another method that will be found highly important in this connection is to take a few moments every day and try to feel that you—the "I Am"—are not only above mind and body, but in a certain sense, distinct from mind and body; in fact, try to isolate the "I Am" for a few moments every day from the rest of your organised being. This practice will give you what may be termed a perfect consciousness of your own individual "I Am," and as you gain that consciousness you will always think of the supreme "I Am" whenever you think of yourself. Accordingly, all your mental actions will, from that time on, come directly from the "I Am"; and if you will continue to stand above all such actions at all times, you will be able to control them and direct them completely.

To examine consciousness and form in this connection is hardly necessary, except to define briefly their general nature, so that we may have a clear idea of what we are dealing with in the conscious field as well as in the field of expression. The "I Am" is fundamentally conscious: that is, the "I Am" knows what exists in the human field or in the human sphere and what is taking place in the human sphere; and that constitutes consciousness. In brief, you are conscious when you know that you exist and have some definite idea as to what is taking place in your sphere of existence. What we speak of as form, is everything in the organised personality that has shape and that serves in any manner to give expression to the forces within us.

In the exercise of consciousness, we find that the "I Am" employs three fundamental actions. When the "I Am" looks out upon life we have simple consciousness. When the "I Am" looks upon its own position in life we have self consciousness, and when the "I Am" looks up into the vastness of real life we have cosmic consciousness.

In simple consciousness, you are only aware of those things that exist externally to yourself, but when you begin to become conscious of yourself as a distinct en tity, you begin to develop self consciousness. When you begin to turn your attention to the great within and begin to look up into the real source of all things, you become conscious of that world that seemingly exists within all worlds, and when you enter upon this experience, you are on the borderland of cosmic consciousness, the most fascinating subject that has ever been known.

When we come to define body, mind and soul, we must, as previously stated, reverse the usual definition. In the past, we have constantly used the expression,

"I have a soul," which naturally implies the belief that "I am a body"; and so deeply has this idea become fixed in the average mind that nearly everybody thinks of the body whenever the term "me" or "myself" is employed. But in this attitude of mind the individual is not above the physical states of thought and feeling; in fact, he is more or less submerged in what may be called a bundle of physical facts and ideas, of which he has very little control. You cannot control anything in your life, however, until you are above it. You cannot control what is in your body until you realize that you are above your body. You cannot control what is in your mind until you realize that you are above your mind, and therefore no one can use the forces within them to any extent so long as they think of themselves as being the body, or as being localised exclusively in the body.

When we examine the whole nature of man, we find that the soul is the man himself, and that the ego is the central principle of the soul; or to use another expression, the soul, including the **"I Am,"** constitutes the individuality, and that visible something through which individuality finds expression, constitutes the personality.

If you wish to understand your forces, and gain that masterful attitude necessary to the control of your forces, train yourself to think that you are a soul, but do not think of the soul as something vague or mysterious. Think of the soul as being the individual you and all that that expression can possibly imply. Train yourself to think that you are master of mind and body, because you are above mind and body, and possess the power to use everything that is in mind and body.

Man is ever in search of strength. It is the strong man that wins. It is the man with power that scales the heights. To be strong is to be great; and it is the privilege of greatness to satisfy every desire, every aspiration, every need. But strength is not for the few alone; it is for all, and the way to strength is simple. Proceed this very moment to the mountain tops of the strength you now possess, and whatever may happen do not come down. Do not weaken under adversity. Resolve to remain as strong, as determined and as highly enthused during the darkest night of adversity as you are during the sunniest day of prosperity. Do not feel disappointed when things seem disappointing. Keep the eye single upon the same brilliant future regardless of circumstances, conditions or events. Do not lose heart when things go wrong. Continue undisturbed in your original resolve to make all things go right. To be overcome by adversity and threatening failure is to lose strength; to always remain in the same lofty, determined mood is to constantly grow in strength. The man who never weakens when things are against him will grow stronger and stronger until all things will delight to be for him. He will finally have all the strength he may desire or need. Be always strong and you will always be stronger.

II
HOW WE GOVERN THE FORCES WE POSSESS

WHENEVER you think or whenever you feel, whenever you speak, whenever you act, or whatever may be taking place in your life, your supreme idea should be that you are above it all, superior to it all, and have control of it all. You simply must take this higher ground in all action, thought and consciousness before you can control yourself and direct, for practical purposes, the forces you possess. Therefore, what has been said in connection with the "I Am," the soul and the individuality as being one, and as standing at the apex of human existence, is just as important as anything that may be said hereafter in connection with the application of the forces in man to practical action. And though this phase of the subject may appear to be somewhat abstract, we shall find no difficulty in understanding it more fully as we apply the ideas evolved. In fact, when we learn to realize that we, by nature, occupy a position that is above mind and body, this part of the subject will be found more interesting than anything else, and its application more profitable.

We can define individuality more fully by stating that it is the invisible man and that everything in man that is invisible belongs to his individuality. It is the individuality that initiates, that controls or directs. Therefore to control and use a force in your own system, you must understand and develop individuality. Your individuality must be made distinct, determined and positive. You must constantly know what you are and what you want, and you must constantly be determined to secure what you want. It is individuality that makes you different from all other organised entities, and it is a highly developed individuality that gives you the power to stand out distinct above the mass, and it is the degree of individuality that you possess that determines largely what position you are to occupy in the world.

Whenever you see a man who is different, who seems to stand out distinct, and who has something vital about him that no one else seems to possess, you have someone whose individuality is highly developed, and you also have someone who is going to make his mark in the world. Take two men of equal power, ability and efficiency, but with this difference. In the one individuality is highly developed, while in the other it is not. You know at once which one of these two is going to reach the highest places in the world of achievement; and the reason is that the one who possesses individuality lives above mind and body, thereby being able to control and direct the forces and powers of mind and body. The man, however, whose individuality is weak, lives more or less down in mind and body, and instead of controlling mind and body, is constantly being influenced by everything from the outside that may enter their consciousness.

Whenever you find a man or a woman who is doing something worthwhile, who is creating an impression upon the race, who is moving forward towards greater and better things, you find the individuality strong, positive and highly developed. It is therefore absolutely necessary that you give your best attention to the development of a strong, positive individuality if you wish to succeed in the world and make the best use of the forces in your possession. A negative or weak individuality drifts with the stream of environment, and usually receives only what others choose to give, but a firm, strong, positive, well-developed individuality, actually controls the ship of their life and destiny, and sooner or later will gain possession of what they originally set out to secure. A positive individuality has

9

the power to take hold of things and turn them to good account. This is one reason why such an individuality always succeeds. Another reason is that the more fully your individuality is developed, the more you are admired by everybody with whom you may come in contact. The human race loves power, and counts it a privilege to give lofty positions to those who have power, and every man or woman whose individuality is highly developed, does possess power—usually exceptional power.

To develop individuality, the first essential is to give the "I Am" its true and lofty position in your mind. The "I Am" is the very centre of individuality, and the more fully conscious you become of the "I Am" the more of the power that is in the "I Am" you arouse, and it is the arousing of this power that makes individuality positive and strong. Another essential is to practise the idea of feeling or conceiving yourself as occupying the masterful attitude. Whenever you think of yourself, think of yourself as being and living and acting in the masterful attitude. Then in addition, make every desire positive, make every feeling positive, make every thought positive, and make every action of mind positive. To make your wants distinct and positive, that is, to actually and fully know what you want and then proceed to want what you want with all the power that is in you, will also tend to give strength and positiveness to your individuality; and the reason is that such actions of mind will tend to place in positive, constructive action every force that is in your system.

A most valuable method is to picture in your mind your own best idea of what a strong, well-developed individuality would necessarily be, and then think of yourself as becoming more and more like that picture. In this connection it is well to remember that we gradually grow into the likeness of that which we think of the most. Therefore, if you have a very clear idea of a highly developed individuality, and think a great deal of that individuality with a strong, positive desire to develop such an individuality, you will gradually and surely move towards that lofty ideal.

Another valuable method is to give conscious recognition to what may be called the bigger man on the inside. Few people think of this greater man that is within them, but we cannot afford to neglect this interior entity for a moment. This greater or larger man is not something that is separate and distinct from ourselves. It is simply the sum-total of the greater powers and possibilities that are within us. We should recognize these, think of them a great deal, and desire with all the power of heart and mind and soul to arouse and express more and more of these inner powers. Thus we shall find that the interior man, our real individuality, will become stronger and more active, and our power to apply our greater possibilities will increase accordingly. The value of individuality is so great that it cannot possibly be overestimated. Every known method that will develop individuality, therefore, should be applied faithfully, thoroughly and constantly. In fact, no one other thing we can do will bring greater returns.

The personality is the visible man. Everything that is visible in the human entity belongs to the personality, but it is more than the body. To say that someone has a fine personality may and may not mean that that personality is beautiful, in the ordinary sense of the term. There might be no physical beauty and yet the personality might be highly developed. There might be nothing striking about such a personality, and yet there would be something extremely attractive, something to greatly admire. On the other hand, when the personality is not well developed, there is nothing in the visible man that you can see, besides ordinary human clay. Everything existing in such a personality is crude and even gross; but there is no excuse for any personality being crude, unrefined or undeveloped. There is not a single personality that cannot be so refined and perfected as to become strikingly attractive, and there are scores of reasons why such development should be sought. The most important reason is that all the forces of man act through the personality, and the finer the personality, the more easily can we direct and express the forces we possess. When the personality is crude, we find it difficult to apply in practical life the finer elements that are within us, and here we find one reason why talent or ability so frequently fails to be its best. In such cases the personality has been neglected, and is not a fit instrument through which finer things and greater things can find expression. The personality is related to the individual as the piano is to the musician. If the piano is out of tune the musician will fail no matter how much of a musician they may be; and likewise, if the piano or instrument is crude in construction, the finest music cannot be expressed through it as a channel. To develop the personality, the principal essential is to learn how to transmute all the creative energies that are generated in the human system, a subject that will be given thorough attention in another chapter.

When we proceed to apply the forces within us, we find three fields of action. The first is the conscious field, the field in which the mind acts when we are awake. The second field is the subconscious, that field in which the mind acts when it goes beneath consciousness. It is also the field in which we act when asleep. The term, "falling asleep," is therefore literally true, as when we go to sleep, the ego goes down, so to speak, into another world—a world so vast, that only portions of it have thus far been explored. The third field is the super-conscious, the field in which the mind acts when it touches the upper realm, and it is when acting in this field that we gain real power and real inspiration; in fact, when we touch the super-conscious, we frequently feel as if we have become more than mere man. To know how to act in the super-conscious field, is therefore highly important, even though the idea may at first sight seem to be vague and somewhat mystical.

We are constantly in touch, however, with the super-conscious whether we know it or not. We frequently enter the super-conscious when we listen to inspiring music, when we read some book that touches the finer intellect, when we listen to someone who speaks from what may be termed the inner throne of authority, when we witness some soul-stirring scene in nature. We also touch the super-conscious when we are carried away with some tremendous ambition, and herein we find practical value in a great measure. When men of tremendous ambition are carried away, so to speak, with the power of that ambition, they almost invariably reach the higher and finer state of mind—a state where they not only feel more power and determination than they ever felt before, but a state in which the mind becomes so extremely active that it almost invariably gains the necessary brilliancy to work out those plans or ideas that are required in order that the ambition may be realized.

It can readily be demonstrated that we get our best ideas from this lofty realm, and it is a well-known fact that no one ever accomplishes great or wonderful things in the world, without touching frequently this sublime inspiring state. When we train the mind to touch the super-conscious at frequent intervals, we always find the ideas we want. We always succeed in providing the ways and means required. No matter what the difficulties may be, we invariably discover something by which we may overcome and conquer completely.

Whenever you find yourself in what may be termed a difficult position, proceed at once to work your mind up into higher and higher attitudes, until you touch the super-conscious, and when you touch that lofty state you will soon receive the ideas or the methods that you need. But this is not the only value connected with the super-conscious. The highest forces in man are the most powerful, but we cannot use those higher forces without acting through the super-conscious field. Therefore, if you want to understand and apply all the forces you possess, you must train the mind to act through the super-conscious as well as the conscious and the subconscious.

However, we must not permit ourselves to live exclusively in this lofty state; though it is the source of the higher forces in man, those forces that are indispensable to the doing of great and important things; nevertheless, those forces cannot be applied unless they are brought down to earth, so to speak, and united with practical action. He who lives exclusively in the super-conscious, will dream wonderful dreams, but if he does not unite the forces of the super-conscious with practical action, he will do nothing else but dream dreams, and those dreams will not come true. It is when we combine mental action in the conscious, subconscious and super-conscious, that we get the results we desire. In brief, it is the full use of all the forces in mind through all the channels of expression that leads to the highest attainment and the greatest achievements.

When we proceed with the practical application of any particular force, we shall not find it necessary to cause that force to act through what may be termed the psychological field, and the reason is that the psychological field in man is the real field of action. It is the field through which the undercurrents flow, and we all understand that it is these undercurrents that determine, not only the direction of action, but the results that follow action. This idea is well illustrated in the following lines:

> "Straws upon the surface flow;
> He who would seek for pearls must dive below."

The term "below" as applied to the life and consciousness of man, is synonymous with the psychological field, or the field of the undercurrents. Ordinary minds skim over the surface. Great minds invariably sound these deeper depths, and act in and through the psychological field. Their minds dive below into the rich vast-ness of what may be termed the gold mines of the mind, and the diamond fields of the soul.

When we enter the psychological field of any force, which simply means the inner and finer field of action of that force, we act through the undercurrents, and thereby proceed to control those currents. It is in the field of the undercurrents that we find both the origin and the action of cause, whether physical or mental. It is these currents, when acted upon intelligently, that remove what we do not want and produce those changes that we do want. They invariably produce effects, both physical and mental, according to the action that we give to them, and all those things that pertain to the personality will respond only to the actions of those currents; that is, you cannot produce any effect in any part of the mind or body unless you first direct the undercurrents of the system to produce those effects. To act through the undercurrents therefore is absolutely necessary, no matter what we may wish to do, or what forces we may wish to control, direct or apply; and we act upon those undercurrents only when we enter the psychological field.

In like manner, we can turn to good account all things in practical everyday life only when we understand the psychology of those things. The reason is, that when we understand the psychology of anything, we understand the power that is back of that particular thing, and that controls it and gives it definite action. In consequence, when we understand the psychology of anything in our own field of action or in our own environment, we will know how to deal with it so as to secure whatever results that particular thing has the power to produce. But this law is especially important in dealing with forces whether those forces act through the mind or through any one of the faculties, through the personality or through the conscious, subconscious or super-conscious fields. In brief, whatever we do in trying to control and direct the powers we possess, we must enter the deeper life of those powers, so that we can get full control of the undercurrents. It is the way those undercurrents flow that determines results, and as we can direct those currents in any way that we desire, we naturally conclude that we can secure whatever results we desire.

Man lives to move forward, To move forward is to live more. To live more is to be more and do more; and it is being and doing that constitutes the path to happiness. The more you are the more you do, the richer your life, the greater your joy. But being and doing must always live together as one. To try to be much and not try to do much is to find life a barren waste. To try to do much and not try to be much is to find life a burden too heavy and wearisome to bear. The being of much gives the necessary inspiration and the necessary power to the doing of much. The doing of much gives the necessary expression to the being of much. And it is the bringing forth of being through the act of doing that produces happiness that is happiness. Being much gives capacity for doing much. Doing much gives expression to the richest and the best that is within us. And the more we increase the richness of that which is within us, the more we increase our happiness, provided we increase, in the same proportion, the expression of that greater richness. The first essential is provided for by the being of much; the second, by the doing of much; and the secret of both may be found by him who lives to move forward.

A WOMAN CLOTHED WITH THE SUN

III
THE USE OF MIND IN PRACTICAL ACTION

I N the present age, it is the power of mind that rules the world, and therefore it is evident that he who has acquired the best use of the power of mind, will realize the greatest success, and reach the highest places that attainment and achievement hold in store. The man who wins is the man who can apply in practical life every part of his mental ability, and who can make every action of his mind tell.

We sometimes wonder why there are so many capable men and admirable women who do not reach those places in life that they seem to deserve, but the answer is simple. They do not apply the power of mind as they should. Their abilities and qualities are either misdirected or applied only in part. These people, however, should not permit themselves to become dissatisfied with fate, but should remember that every individuality who learns to make full use of the power of their mind will reach their goal; they will realize their desire and will positively win.

There are several reasons why, though the principle reason is found in the fact that when the power of the mind is used correctly in working out what we wish to accomplish, the other forces we possess are readily applied for the same purpose, and this fact becomes evident when we realise that the power of mind is not only the ruling power in the world, but is also the ruling power in man himself. All other faculties in man are ruled by the power of his mind. It is the action of his mind that determines the action of all the other forces in his possession. Therefore, to secure the results desired, he must give his first thought to the scientific and constructive application of mental action.

In a preceding chapter, it was stated that the "I Am" is the ruling principle in man, and from that statement the conclusion may be drawn that the "I Am" is the ruling power as well, but this is not strictly correct. There is a difference between principle and power, though for practical purposes it is not necessary to consider the abstract phase of this difference. All that is necessary is to realize that the "I Am" directs the mind, and that the power of the mind directs and controls everything else in the human system. It is the mind that occupies the throne but the "I Am" is the power behind the throne.

This being true, it becomes highly important to understand how the power of the mind should be used, but before we can understand the use of this power, we must learn what this power actually is. Generally speaking, we may say that the power of mind is the sum-total of all the forces of the mental world, including those forces that are employed in the process of thinking. The power of mind includes the power of the will, the power of desire, the power of feeling, and the power of thought. It includes conscious action in all its phases and subconscious action in all its phases; in fact, it includes anything and everything that is placed in action through the mind, by the mind or in the mind.

To use the power of the mind, the first essential is to direct every mental action toward the goal in view, and this direction must not be occasional, but constant. Most minds, however, do not apply this law. They think about a certain thing one moment, and about something else the next moment. At a certain hour their mental actions work along a certain line, and at the next hour those actions work along a different line. Sometimes the goal in view is one thing, and sometimes another, so the actions of the mind do not move constantly toward a certain definite goal, but are mostly scattered. We know, however, that every individual

15

who is actually working themselves steadily and surely toward the goal they have in view, invariably directs all the power of their thought upon that goal. In their mind not a single mental action is thrown away, not a single mental force wasted. All the power that is in them is being directed to work for what they wish to accomplish, and the reason that every power responds in this way is because they are not thinking of one thing now and something else the next moment. They are thinking all the time of what they wish to attain and achieve. The full power of mind is turned upon that object, and as mind is the ruling power, the full power of all their other forces will tend to work for the same object.

In using the power of mind as well as all the other forces we possess, the first question to answer is what we really want, or what we really want to accomplish; and when this question is answered, the one thing that is wanted should be fixed so clearly in thought that it can be seen by the mind's eye every minute. But the majority do not know what they really want. They may have some vague desire, but they have not determined clearly, definitely and positively what they really want, and this is one of the principal causes of failure. So long as we do not know definitely what we want, our forces will be scattered, and so long as our forces are scattered, we will accomplish but little, or fail entirely. When we know what we want, however, and proceed to work for it with all the power and ability that is in us, we may rest assured that we will get it. When we direct the power of thinking, the power of will, the power of mental action, the power of desire, the power of ambition, in fact, all the power we possess on the one thing we want, on the one goal we desire to reach, it is not difficult to understand why success in a greater and greater measure must be realized.

To illustrate this subject further, we will suppose that you have a certain ambition and continue to concentrate your thought and the power of your mind upon that ambition every minute for an indefinite period, with no cessation whatever. The result will be that you will gradually and surely train all the forces within you to work for the realization of that ambition, and in the course of time, the full capacity of your entire mental system will be applied in working for that particular thing.

On the other hand, suppose you do as most people do under average circumstances. Suppose, after you have given your ambition a certain amount of thought, you come to the conclusion that possibly you might succeed better along another line. Then you begin to direct the power of your mind along that other line. Later on, you come to the conclusion that there is still another channel through which you might succeed, and you proceed accordingly to direct your mind upon this third ambition. Then what will happen? Simply this: You will make three good beginnings, but in every case you will stop before you have accomplished anything. There are thousands of capable men and women, however, who make this mistake every year of their lives. The full force of their mental system is directed upon a certain ambition only for a short time; then it is directed elsewhere. They never continue long enough along any particular line to secure results from their efforts, and therefore results are never secured.

Then there are other minds who give most of their attention to a certain ambition and succeed fairly well, but give the rest of their attention to a number of minor ambitions that have no particular importance. Thus they are using only a fraction of their power in a way that will tell. The rest of it is thrown away along a number of lines through which nothing is gained. But in this age efficiency is demanded everywhere in world's work, and anyone who wants to occupy a place

16

that will satisfy their ambition and desire, cannot afford to waste even a small part of the power they may possess. They need it all along the line of their leading ambition, and therefore should not permit counter attractions to occupy their mind for a moment.

If you have a certain ambition or a certain desire, think about that ambition at all times. Keep that ambition before your mind constantly, and do not hesitate to make your ambition as high as possible. The higher you aim, the greater will be your achievements, though that does not necessarily mean that you will realize your highest aims as fully as you have pictured them in your mind; but the fact is that those who have low aims, usually realize what is even below their aims, while those who have high aims usually realize very nearly, if not fully, what their original ambition calls for. The principle is to direct the power of mind upon the very highest, the very largest and the very greatest mental conception of that which we intend to achieve. The first essential therefore, is to direct the full power of mind and thought upon the goal in view, and to continue to direct the mind in that manner every minute, regardless of circumstances or conditions.

The second essential is to make every mental action positive. When we desire certain things or when we think of certain things we wish to attain or achieve, the question should be if our mental attitudes at the time are positive or negative. To answer this we only have to remember that every positive action always goes toward that which receives its attention, while a negative action always retreats. A positive action is an action that you feel when you realize that every force in your entire system is pushed forward, so to speak, and that it is passing through what may be termed an expanding and enlarging state of feeling or consciousness. The positive attitude of mind is also indicated by the feeling of a firm, determined fulness throughout the nervous system. When every nerve feels full, strong and determined, you are in the positive attitude, and whatever you may do at the time will produce results along the line of your desire or your ambition. When you are in a positive state of mind you are never nervous or disturbed, you are never agitated or strenuous; in fact, the more positive you are the deeper your calmness and the better your control over your entire system.

The positive man is not one who rushes helter-skelter here and there regardless of judgement or constructive action, but one who is absolutely calm and controlled under every circumstance, and yet so thoroughly full of energy that every atom in his being is ready, under every circumstance, to accomplish and achieve. This energy is not permitted to act, however, until the proper time arrives, and then its action goes directly to the goal in view.

The positive mind is always in harmony with itself, while the negative mind is always out of harmony, and thereby loses the greater part of its power. Positiveness always means strength stored up, power held in the system under perfect control, until the time of action; and during the time of action directed constructively under the same perfect control. In the positive mind, all the actions of the mental system are working in harmony and are being fully directed toward the object in view, while in the negative mind, those same actions are scattered, restless, nervous, disturbed, moving here and there, sometimes under direction, but most of the time not. That the one should invariably succeed is therefore just as evident as that the other should invariably fail. Scattered energy cannot do otherwise but fail, while positively directed energy simply must succeed. A positive mind is like a powerful stream of water that is gathering volume and force from hundreds of tributaries all along its course. The further on it goes the greater its power, until when it reaches its goal, that power is simply immense. A negative mind, however, would be something like a stream, that the further it flows the more divisions it makes, until, when it reaches its goal, instead of being one powerful stream, it has become a hundred small, weak, shallow streams.

To develop positiveness it is necessary to cultivate those qualities that constitute positiveness. Make it a point to give your whole attention to what you want to accomplish, and give that attention firmness, calmness and determination. Try to give depth to every desire until you feel as if all the powers of your system were acting, not on the surface, but from the greater world within. As this attitude is cultivated, positiveness will become more and more distinct, until you can actually feel yourself gaining power and prestige. And the effect will not only be noticed in your own ability to better direct and apply your talents, but others will discover the change. Accordingly, those who are looking for people of power, people who can do things, will look to you as the one to occupy the position that has to be filled.

Positiveness therefore, not only gives you the ability to make a far better use of the forces you possess, but it also gives you personality, that much admired something that will most surely cause you to be selected where people of power are needed. The world does not care for negative personalities. Such personalities look weak and empty, and are usually ignored, but everybody is attracted to a positive personality; and it is the positive personality that is always given the preference. Nor is this otherwise but right, because the positive personality has better use of their power, and therefore is able to act with greater efficiency wherever they are called upon to act.

The third essential in the right use of the mind is to make every mental action constructive, and a constructive mental action is one that is based upon a deep seated desire to develop, to increase, to achieve, to attain—in brief, to become larger and greater, and to do something of far greater worth than has been done before. If you will cause every mental action you entertain to have that feeling, constructiveness will soon became second nature to your entire mental system; that is, all the forces of your mind will begin to become building forces, and will continue to build you up along any line through which you may desire to act.

Inspire your mind constantly with a building desire, and make this desire so strong that very part of your system will constantly feel that it wants to become greater, more capable and more efficient. An excellent practice in this connection is to try to enlarge upon all your ideas of things whenever you have spare moments for real thought. This practice will tend to produce a growing tendency in every process of your thinking. Another good practice is to inspire every mental action with more ambition. We cannot have too much ambition. We may have too much aimless ambition, but we cannot have too much real constructive ambition. If your ambition is very strong, and is directed toward something definite, every action of your mind, every action of your personality, and every action of your faculties will become constructive; that is, all those actions will be inspired by the tremendous force of your ambition to work for the realization of that ambition.

Never permit restless ambition. Whenever you feel the force of ambition, direct your mind at once in a calm, determined manner upon that which you really want to accomplish in life. Make this a daily practice, and you will steadily train all your faculties and powers not only to work for the realization of that ambition, but become more and more efficient in that direction. Before long your forces and faculties will be sufficiently competent to accomplish what you want.

18

In the proper use of the mind therefore, these three essentials should be applied constantly and thoroughly. First, direct all the powers of mind, all the powers of thought, and all your thinking upon the goal you have in view. Second, train every mental action to be deeply and calmly positive. Third, train every mental action to be constructive, to be filled with a building spirit, to be inspired with a ceaseless desire to develop the greater, to achieve the greater, to attain the greater. When you have acquired these three, you will begin to use your forces in such a way that results must follow. You will begin to move forward steadily and surely, and you will be constantly gaining ground. Your mind will have become like the stream mentioned above. It will gather volume and force as it moves on and on, until finally that volume will be great enough to remove any obstacle in its way, and that force powerful enough to do anything you may have in view.

In order to apply these three essentials in the most effective manner, there are several misuses of the mind that must be avoided. Avoid the forceful, the aggressive, and the domineering attitudes, and do not permit your mind to become intense, unless it is under perfect control. Never attempt to control or influence others in any way whatever. You will seldom succeed in that manner, and when you do, the success will be temporary; besides, such a practice always weakens your mind. Do not turn the power of your mind upon others, but turn it upon yourself in such a way that it will make you stronger, more positive, more capable, and more efficient, and as you develop in this manner, success must come of itself. There is only one way by which you can influence others legitimately and that is through the giving of instruction, but in that case, there is no desire to influence. You desire simply to impart knowledge and information, and you exercise a most desirable influence without desiring to do so.

A great many men and women, after discovering the immense power of mind, have come to the conclusion that they might change circumstances by exercising mental power upon those circumstances in some mysterious manner, but such a practice means nothing but a waste of energy. The way to control circumstances is to control the forces within yourself to make a greater human being of yourself, and as you become greater and more competent, you will naturally gravitate into better circumstances. In this connection, we should remember that like attracts like. If you want that which is better, make yourself better. If you want to realize the ideal, make yourself more ideal. If you want better friends, make yourself a better friend. If you want to associate with people of worth, make yourself more worthy. If you want to meet that which is agreeable, make yourself more agreeable. If you want to enter conditions and circumstances that are more pleasing, make yourself more pleasing. In brief, whatever you want, produce that something in yourself, and you will positively gravitate towards the corresponding conditions in the external world. But to improve yourself along those lines, it is necessary to apply for that purpose, all the power you possess. You cannot afford to waste any of it, and every misuse of the mind will waste power.

Avoid all destructive attitudes of the mind, such an anger, hatred, malice, envy, jealousy, revenge, depression, discouragement, disappointment, worry, fear, and so on. Never antagonise, never resist what is wrong, and never try to get even. Make the best use of your own talent and the best that is in store for you will positively come your way. When others seem to take advantage of you, do not retaliate by trying to take advantage of them. Use your power in improving yourself, so that you can do better and better work. That is how you are going to win in the race. Later on, those who tried to take advantage of you will be left in the rear. Remember, those who are dealing unjustly with you or with anybody are misusing their mind. They are therefore losing their power, and will, in the course of time, begin to lose ground; but if you, in the mean time, are turning the full power of your mind to good account, you will not only gain more power, but you will soon begin to gain ground. You will gain and continue to gain in the long run, while others who have been misusing their minds will lose mostly everything in the long run. That is how you are going to win, and win splendidly regardless of ill treatment or opposition.

A great many people imagine that they can promote their own success by trying to prevent the success of other, but it is one of the greatest delusions in the world. If you want to promote your own success as thoroughly as your capacity will permit, take an active interest in the success of everybody, because this will not only keep your mind in the success attitude and cause you to think success all along the line, but it will enlarge your mind so as to give you a greater and better grasp upon the fields of success. If you are trying to prevent the success of others, you are acting in the destructive attitude, which sooner or later will react on others, but if you are taking an active interest in the success of everybody, you are entertaining only constructive attitudes, and these will sooner or later accumulate in your own mind to add volume and power to the forces of success that you are building up in yourself.

In this connection, we may well ask why those succeed who do succeed, why so many succeed only in part, and why so many fail utterly. These are questions that occupy the minds of most people, and hundreds of answers have been given, but there is only one answer that goes to rock bottom. Those people who fail, and who continue to fail all along the line, fail because the power of their minds is either in a habitual negative state, or is always misdirected. If the power of mind is not working positively and constructively for a certain goal, you are not going to succeed. If your mind is not positive, it is negative, and negative minds float with the stream. We must remember that we are in the midst of all kinds of circumstances, some of which are for us and some of which are against us, and we will either have to make our own way or drift, and if we drift we go wherever the stream goes. But most of the streams of human life are found to float in the world of the ordinary and the inferior. Therefore, if you drift, you will drift with the inferior, and your goal will be failure.

When we analyse the minds of people who have failed, we invariably find that they are either negative, non-constructive or aimless. Their forces are scattered, and what is in them is seldom applied constructively. There is an emptiness about their personality that indicates negativeness. There is an uncertainty in their facial expression that indicates the absence of definite ambition. There is nothing of a positive, determined nature going on in their mental world. They have not taken definite action along any line. They are dependent upon fate and circumstances. They are drifting with some stream, and that they should accomplish little if anything is inevitable. This does not mean, however, that their mental world is necessarily unproductive; in fact, those very minds are in many instances immensely rich with possibilities. The trouble is, those possibilities continue to be dormant, and what is in them is not being brought forth and trained for definite action or actual results.

What those people should do, is to proceed at once to comply with the three essentials mentioned above, and before many months there will be a turn in the lane. They will soon cease to drift, and will then begin to make their own life, their own circumstances, and their own future.

In this connection, it is well to remember that negative people and non-constructive minds never attract that which is helpful in their circumstances. The more you drift, the more people you meet who also drift, while on the other hand, when you begin to make your own life and become positive, you begin to meet more positive people and more constructive circumstances. This explains why "God helps them that help themselves." When you begin to help yourself, which means to make the best of what is in yourself, you begin to attract to yourself more and more of those helpful things that may exist all about you. In other words, constructive forces attract constructive forces; positive forces attract positive forces. A growing mind attracts elements and forces that help to promote growth, and people who are determined to make more and more of themselves, are drawn more and more into circumstances through which they will find the opportunity to make more of themselves. And this law works not only in connection with the external world, but also the internal world. When you begin to make a positive determined use of those powers in yourself that are already in Positive action, you draw forth into action powers within you that have been dormant, and as this process continues, you will find that you will accumulate volume, capacity and power in your mental world, until you finally become a mental giant.

As you begin to grow and become more capable, you will find that you will meet better and better opportunities, not only opportunities for promoting external success, but opportunities for further building yourself up along the lines of ability, capacity and talent. You thus demonstrate the law that "Nothing succeeds like success," and "To him that hath shall be given." And here it is well to remember that it is not necessary to possess external things in the beginning to be counted among them "that hath.." It is only necessary in the beginning to possess the interior riches; that is, to take control of what is in you, and proceed to use it positively with a definite goal in view. He who has control of his own mind has already great riches. He has sufficient wealth to be placed among those who have. He is already successful, and if he continues as he has begun, his success will soon appear in the external world. Thus the wealth that existed at first in the internal only will take shape and form in the external. This is a law that is unfailing, and there is not a man or woman on the face of the earth that cannot apply it with the most satisfying results.

The reason why so many fail is thus found in the fact that they do not fully and constructively apply the forces and powers they possess, and the reason why so many succeed only to a slight degree is found in the fact that only a small fraction of their power is applied properly. But anyone can learn the full and proper use of all that is in them by applying faithfully the three essentials mentioned above. The reason why those succeed who do succeed is found in the fact that a large measure of their forces and powers is applied according to those three essentials, and as those essentials can be applied by anyone, even to the most perfect degree, there is no reason why all should not succeed.

Sometimes we meet people who have only ordinary ability, but who are very successful. Then we meet others who have great ability but who are not successful, or who succeed only to a slight degree. At first we see no explanation, but when we understand the cause of success as well as the cause of failure, the desired explanation is easily found. The man or woman with ordinary ability, if they comply with the three essentials necessary to the right use of mind, will naturally succeed, though if they had greater ability, their success would of course become greater in proportion. But the individual who has great ability, yet does not apply the three essentials necessary to the right use of mind, cannot succeed.

The positive and constructive use of the power of mind, with a definite goal in view will invariably result in advancement, attainment and achievement, but if we wish to use that power in its full capacity, the action of the mind must be deep. In addition to the right use of the mind, we must also learn the full use of mind, and as the full use implies the use of the whole mind, the deeper mental fields and forces, as well as the usual mental fields and forces, it is necessary to understand the subconscious as well as the conscious.

> *When you think of yourself do not think of that part of yourself that appears on the surface. That part is the smaller part and the lesser should not be pictured in mind. Think of your larger self, the immense subconscious self that is limitless both in power and in possibility.*
>
> *Believe in yourself but not simply in a part of yourself. Give constant recognition to all that is in you, and, in that all have full faith and confidence.*
>
> *Give the bigger being on the inside full right of way. Believe thoroughly in your greater interior self. Know that you have something within you that is greater than any obstacle, circumstance or difficulty that you can possibly meet. Then in the full faith in this greater something, proceed with your work.*

IV
THE FORCES OF THE SUBCONSCIOUS

IN using the power of the mind, the deeper the action of thought, will and desire, the greater the result. Accordingly, all mental action to be strong and effective, must be subconscious; that is, it must act in the field of the mental undercurrent as it is in this field that things are actually done. Those forces that play upon the surface of mind may be changed and turned from their course by almost any outside influence, and their purpose thus averted. But this is never true of the undercurrents. Anything that gets into the mental undercurrents will be seen through to a finish, regardless of external circumstances or conditions; and it is with difficulty that the course of these currents is changed when once they have been placed in full positive action. It is highly important therefore that we permit nothing to take action in these undercurrents that we do not wish to encourage and promote; and for the same reason, it is equally important that we cause everything to take action in these currents that we do wish to encourage and promote.

These undercurrents, however, act only through the subconscious, and are controlled by the subconscious. In consequence, it is the subconscious which we must understand and act upon if we want the power of mind to work with full capacity and produce the greatest measure possible of the results desired.

In defining the subconscious mind, it is first necessary to state that it is not a separate mind. There are not two minds. There is only one mind in man, but it has two phases—the conscious and the subconscious. We may define the conscious as the upper side of the mentality, and the subconscious as the under side. The subconscious may also be defined as a vast mental field permeating the entire objective personality, thereby filling every atom of the personality through and through. We shall come nearer the truth, however, if we think of the subconscious as a finer mental force, having distinct powers, functions and possibilities, or as a great mental sea of life, energy and power, the force and capacity of which has never been measured.

The conscious mind is on the surface, and therefore we act through the conscious mind whenever mental action moves through the surface of thought, will or desire, but whenever we enter into deeper mental action and sound the vast depths of this underlying mental life, we touch the subconscious, though we must remember that we do not become oblivious to the conscious every time we touch the subconscious, as the two are inseparably united. That the two phases of the mind are related can be well illustrated by comparing the conscious mind with a sponge, and the subconscious with the water permeating the sponge. We know that every fibre of the sponge is in touch with the water, and in the same manner, every part of the conscious mind, as well as every atom in the personality, is in touch with the subconscious, and completely filled, through and through, with the life and the force of the subconscious.

It has frequently been stated that the subconscious mind occupies the Fourth Dimension of space, and though this is a matter that cannot be exactly demonstrated, nevertheless, the more we study the nature of the subconscious, as well as the Fourth Dimension, the more convinced we become that the former occupies the field of the latter. This, however, is simply a matter that holds interest in philosophical investigation. Whether the subconscious occupies the Fourth Dimension or some other dimension of space will make no difference as to its practical value.

23

In order to understand the subconscious, it is well at the outset to familiarise ourselves with its natural functions, as this will convince ourselves of the fact that we are not dealing with something that is beyond normal mental action. The subconscious mind controls all the natural functions of the body, such as the circulation, respiration, digestion, assimilation, physical repair, etc. It also controls all the involuntary actions of the body, and all those actions of mind and body that continue their natural movements without direction from the will. The subconscious perpetuates characteristics, traits, and qualities that are peculiar to individuals, species and races. What is called heredity therefore is altogether a subconscious process. The same is true of what is called second nature. Whenever anything has been repeated a sufficient number of times to have become habitual, it becomes second nature, or rather a subconscious action. It frequently happens, however, that a conscious action may become a subconscious action without repetition, and thus becomes second nature almost at once.

When we examine the nature of the subconscious, we find that it responds to almost anything the conscious mind may desire or direct, though it is usually necessary for the conscious mind to express its desire upon the subconscious for some time before the desired response is secured. The subconscious is a most willing servant, and is so competent that thus far we have failed to find a single thing along mental lines that it will not or cannot do. It submits readily to almost any kind of training, and will do practically anything that it is directed to do, whether the thing is to our advantage or not.

In this connection, it is interesting to learn that there are a number of things in the human system usually looked upon as natural, and inevitable, that are simply the results of misdirected subconscious training in the past. We frequently speak of human weaknesses as natural, but weakness is never natural. Although it may appear, it is invariably the result of imperfect subconscious training. It is never natural to go wrong, but it is natural to go right, and the reason why is simple. Every right action is in harmony with natural law, while every wrong action is a violation of natural law.

It has also been stated that the aging process is natural, but modern science has demonstrated that it is not natural for a person to age at sixty, seventy, or eighty years. The fact that the average person does manifest nearly all the conditions of old age at those periods of time, or earlier, simply proves that the subconscious mind has been trained through many generations to produce old age at sixty, seventy, eighty or ninety, as the case may be, and the subconscious always does what it has been trained to do. It can just as readily be trained, however, to produce greater physical strength and greater mental capacity at ninety than we possess at thirty or forty. It can also be trained to possess the same virile youth at one hundred as the healthiest man or woman of twenty may possess. In fact, practically every condition that appears in the mind, the character and the personality of the human race, is the result of what the subconscious mind has been directed to do during past generations. It is therefore evident that as the subconscious is directed to produce different conditions in mind, character, and personality— conditions that are in perfect harmony with the natural law of human development, such conditions will invariably appear in the race. Thus we understand how a new race or a superior race may appear upon this planet.

There are a great many people who are disturbed over the fact that they have inherited certain characteristics or ailments from their parents, but what they have inherited is simply subconscious tendencies in that direction, and those tendencies can be changed absolutely. What we inherit from our parents can be eliminated so completely that no one would ever know it had been there. In like manner, we can improve so decidedly upon the good qualities that we have inherited from our parents that any similarity between parent and child in those respects would disappear completely. The subconscious mind is always ready, willing and competent to make any change for the better in our physical or mental make-up that we may desire, though it does not work in some miraculous manner, nor does it usually produce results instantaneously. In most instances its actions are gradual, but they invariably produce the results intended if the proper training continues.

The subconscious mind will respond to the directions of the conscious mind so long as those directions do not interfere with the absolute laws of nature. The subconscious never moves against natural law, but it has the power to so use natural law that improvement along any line can be secured. It will reproduce in mind and body any condition that is thoroughly impressed and deeply felt by the conscious mind. It will bring forth undesirable conditions when directed to produce such conditions, and it will bring forth health, strength, youth and added power when so directed. If you continue to desire a strong physical body, and fully expect the subconscious to build for you a stronger body, you will find that this will gradually or finally be done. You will steadily grow in physical strength. If you continue to desire greater ability along a certain line and expect the subconscious to produce greater mental power along that line, your ability will increase as expected, but it is necessary in this connection to be persistent and persevering. To become enthusiastic about these things for a few days is not sufficient. It is when we apply these laws persistently for weeks, months and years that we find the results to be, not only what we expected, but frequently far greater.

Everything has a tendency to grow in the subconscious. Whenever an impression or desire is placed in the subconscious, it has a tendency to become larger and therefore the bad becomes worse when it enters the subconscious, while the good becomes better. We have the power, however, to exclude the bad from the subconscious and cause only the good to enter that immense field. Whenever you say that you are tired and permit that feeling to sink into the subconscious, you will almost at once feel more tired. Whenever you feel sick and permit that feeling to enter the subconscious, you always feel worse. The same is true when you are weak, sad, disappointed or depressed. If you let those feelings sink into your subconscious, they will become worse. On the other hand, when we feel happy, strong, persistent and determined, and permit those feelings to enter the subconscious, we always feel better. It is therefore highly important that we positively refuse to give in to any undesirable feeling. Whenever we give in to any feeling, it becomes subconscious, and if that feeling is bad, it becomes worse; but so long as we keep undesirable feelings on the outside, so to speak, we will hold them at bay, until nature can readjust itself or gather reserve force and thus put them out of the way altogether.

We should never give in to sickness, though that does not mean that we should continue to work as hard as usual when not feeling well, or cause mind and body to continue in their usual activities. When we find it necessary, we should give ourselves a complete rest, but we should never give in to the feeling of sickness. The rest that may be taken will help the body to recuperate, and when it does the threatening ailment will disappear. When you feel tired or depressed, do not admit it, but turn your attention at once upon something that is extremely interesting—something that will completely turn your mind towards the pleasing, the more desirable or the ideal. Persist in feeling the way you want to feel, and permit only wholesome feelings to enter the subconscious. Thus wholesome feelings will live and grow, and after awhile your power to feel good at all times will have become so strong that you can put out of the way any adverse feeling that may threaten at any time.

In this connection, we may mention something that holds more than usual interest. It has been stated by those who are in a position to know, that no one dies until they give up; that is, gives in to those adverse conditions that are at work in their system, tending to produce physical death. So long as he or she refuses to give in to those conditions, they continue to live. How long a person could refuse to give in even under the most adverse circumstances is a question, but one thing is certain, that thousands and thousands of deaths could be prevented every year if the patient in each case refused to give in. In many instances, the forces of life and death are almost equally balanced. Which one is going to win depends upon the mental attitude of the patient. If he or she gives over the mind and will to the side of the forces of life, those forces are most likely to win, but if they permit the mind to act with death, the forces of death are most certain to win. So long as one continues to persist in living, refusing absolutely to give into death, they are throwing the full power of mind, thought and will on the side of life. They thereby increase the power of life, and may increase that power sufficiently to overcome death. Again we say that it is a question how many times a person could overcome death by this method, but the fact remains that this method alone can save life repeatedly in the majority of cases; and all will admit after further thought on this subject that the majority will be very large. This is a method, therefore, that deserves the best of attention in every sickroom. No person should be permitted to die until all available methods for prolonging life have been exhausted, and this last mentioned method is one that will accomplish far more than most of us may expect; and its secret is found in the fact that whenever we give in to any condition or action, it becomes stronger, due to the tendency of the subconscious to enlarge, increase and magnify whatever it receives. Give in to the forces of death, and the subconscious mind will increase the powers of that force. Give in to the forces of life, and the subconscious mind will increase the power of your life and you will continue to live.

Concerning the general possibilities of the subconscious, we should remember that every faculty has a subconscious side, and that it becomes larger and more competent as this subconscious side is developed. This being true, it is evident that ability and genius might be developed in any mind even to a remarkable degree, as no limit has been found to the subconscious in any of its forces. In like manner, every cell in the body has a subconscious side, and therefore, if the subconscious side of the personality were developed, we can realize what improvement would become possible in that field. There is a subconscious side to all the faculties in human nature, and if these were developed, we understand how man could become ideal, even far beyond our present dreams of a new race.

It is not well however to give the major portion of our attention to future possibilities. It is what is possible now that we should aim to develop and apply, and present possibilities indicate that improvement along any line, whether it be in working capacity, ability, health, happiness and character can be secured without fail if the subconscious is properly directed.

To direct the subconscious along any line, it is only necessary to desire what

26

you want and to make those desires so deep and so persistent that they become positive forces in the subconscious field. When you feel that you want a certain thing, give in to that feeling and also make that feeling positive. Give in to your ambitions in the same manner, and also to every desire that you wish to realize. Let your thought of all those things that you wish to increase in any line get into your system, because whatever gets into your system, the subconscious will proceed to develop, work out and express.

In using the subconscious, we should remember that we are not using something that is separated from normal life. The difference between the individual who makes scientific use of the subconscious and the one who does not, is simply this; the latter employs only a small part of their mind, while the former employs the whole of their mind. And this explains why those who employ the subconscious intelligently have greater working capacity, greater ability and greater endurance. In consequence they sometimes do the work of two or three people, and do excellent work in addition. To train the subconscious for practical action is therefore a matter of common sense. It is a matter of refusing to cultivate only a small corner of your mental field when you can cultivate the entire field.

When you have made up your mind what you want to do, say to yourself a thousand times a day that you will do it. The best way will soon open. You will have the opportunity you desire.

If you would be greater in the future than you are now, be all that you can be now. He who is his best develops the power to be better. He who lives his ideals is creating a life that actually is ideal.

There is nothing in your life that you cannot modify, change or improve when you learn to regulate your thought.

Our destiny is not mapped out for us by some exterior power; we map it out for ourselves. What we think and do in the present determines what shall happen to us in the future.

V
TRAINING THE SUBCONSCIOUS FOR PRACTICAL RESULTS

WHEN we proceed to train the subconscious along any line, or for special results, we must always comply with the following law: The subconscious responds to the impressions, the suggestions, the desires, the expectations and the directions of the conscious mind, provided that the conscious touches the subconscious at the time. The secret therefore is found in the two phases of the mind touching each other as directions are being made; and to cause the conscious to touch the subconscious, it is necessary to feel conscious action penetrating your entire interior system; that is, you should feel at the time that you are living not simply on the surface, but through and through. At such times, the mind should be calm and in perfect poise, and should be conscious of that finer, greater something within you that has greater depth than mere surface existence.

When you wish to direct the subconscious to produce physical health, first picture in your mind a clear idea of perfect health. Try to see this idea with the mind's eye, and then try to feel the meaning of this idea with consciousness, and while you are in the attitude of that feeling, permit your thought and your attention to pass into that deep quiet, serene state of being wherein you can feel the mental idea of wholeness and health entering into the very life of every atom in your system. In brief, try to feel perfectly healthy in your mind and then let that feeling sink into your entire physical system. Whenever you feel illness coming on, you can nip it in the bud by this simple method, because if the subconscious is directed to produce more health, added forces of health will soon begin to come forth from within, and put out of the way, so to speak, any disorder or ailment that may be on the verge of getting a foothold in the body. Always remember that whatever is impressed on the subconscious will after a while be expressed from the subconscious into the personality; and where the physical conditions that you wish to remove are only slight, enough subconscious power can be aroused to restore immediate order, harmony and wholeness. When the condition you wish to remove has continued for some time, however, repeated efforts may be required to cause the subconscious to act in the matter. But one thing is certain, that if you continue to direct the subconscious to remove that condition, it positively will be removed.

The subconscious does not simply posses the power to remove undesirable conditions from the physical or mental state. It can also produce those better conditions that we may want, and develop further those desirable conditions that we already possess. To apply the law for this purpose, deeply desire those conditions that you do want, and have a very clear idea in your mind as to what you want those conditions to be. In giving the subconscious directions for anything desired in our physical or mental makeup, we should always have improvement in mind, as the subconscious always does the best work when we are thoroughly filled with the desire to do better. If we want health, we should direct the subconscious to produce more and more health. If we want power, we should direct the subconscious not simply to give us a great deal or a certain amount of power, but to give us more and more power. In this manner, we shall secure results from the very beginning. If we try to train the subconscious to produce a certain amount, it might be some time before that amount can be developed. In the meantime, we should meet disappointment and delay, but if our desire is for steady increase along all lines from where we stand now, we shall be able to secure, first, a slight improvement and then added improvement to be followed with still greater improvement until we finally reach the highest goal we have in view.

No effort should be made to destroy those qualities that we may not desire. Whatever we think about deeply or intensely, the subconscious will take up and develop further. Therefore, if we think about our failings, shortcomings or bad habits, the subconscious will take them up and give them more life and activity than they ever had before. If there is anything in our nature therefore that we wish to change, we should simply proceed to build up what we want and forget completely what we wish to eliminate. When the good develops, the bad disappears. When the greater is built up, the lesser will either be removed or completely transformed and combined with the greater.

That the subconscious can increase your ability and your capacity is a fact that is readily demonstrated. Whenever the subconscious mind is aroused, mental power and working capacity are invariably increased sometimes to such an extent that the individual seems to be possessed with a super human power. We all know of instances where great things were accomplished simply through the fact that the individual was carried on and on by an immense power within them that seemed to be distinct from themselves and greater than themselves; but it was simply the greater powers of the subconscious that were aroused and placed in positive, determined action. These instances, however, need not be exceptions. Any man, under any circumstances, can so increase the power of his mind, his thought and his will as to be actually carried away with the same tremendous force; that is, the power within him becomes so strong that he is actually pushed through to the goal he has in view regardless of circumstances, conditions or obstacles.

This being true, we should arouse the subconscious no matter what it is we have to do. No day is complete unless we begin that day by making alive everything that we possess in our whole mind, conscious and subconscious. Whenever you have work to do at some future time, direct the subconscious to increase your ability and capacity at the time specified, and fully expect the desired increase to be secured. If you want new ideas on certain studies or new plans in your work, direct the subconscious to produce them and you will get them without fail. The moment the direction is given, the subconscious will go to work along that line; and in this connection, we should remember that though we may fail to get the idea desired through the conscious mind alone, it is quite natural that we should get it when we also enlist the subconscious, because the whole mind is much greater, far more capable and far more resourceful than just a small part of the mind.

When demands are urgent, the subconscious responds more readily, especially when feelings at the time are also very deep. When you need certain results, say that you must have them, and put your whole energy into the "must." Whatever you make up your mind that you must do, you will in some manner get the power to do.

There are a number of instances on record where people were carried through certain events by what seemed to be a miraculous power, but the cause of it all was simply this—that they had to do it, and whatever you have to do, the subconscious mind will invariably give you the power to do. The reason for this is found in the fact that when you feel that you must do a thing and that you have to do it, your desires are so strong and so deep that they go into the very depths of the subconscious and thus call to action the full power of that vast interior realm.

If you have some great ambition that you wish to realize, direct the subconscious several times each day and each night before you go to sleep, to work out the necessary ways and means; and if you are determined, those ways and means will be forthcoming. But here it is necessary to remember that we must concentrate on the one thing wanted. If your mind scatters, sometimes giving attention to one ambition and sometimes to another, you will confuse the subconscious and the ways and means desired will not be secured. Make your ambition a vital part of your life, and try to feel the force of that ambition every single moment of your existence. If you do this, your ambition will certainly be realized. It may take a year, it may take five years, it may take ten years or more, but your ambition will be realized. This being true, no one need feel disturbed about the future, because if they actually know what they want to accomplish, and train the subconscious to produce the idea, the methods, the necessary ability and the required capacity, all these things will be secured.

If there is any condition from which you desire to secure emancipation, direct the subconscious to give you that information through which you may find a way out. The subconscious can. We all remember the saying, "Where there is a will there is a way," and it is true, because when you actually will to do a certain thing, the power of the mind becomes so deep and so strong along that line, that the entire subconscious mind is put to work on the case, so to speak; and under such circumstances, the way will always be found. When you put your whole mind, conscious and subconscious, to work on any problem, you will find the solution. If there is any talent that you wish to develop further, direct the subconscious every day, and as frequently as possible, to enlarge the inner life of that talent and to increase its brilliancy and power.

When you are about to undertake anything new, do not proceed until you have submitted the proposition to the subconscious, and here we find the real value of "sleeping over" new plans before we finally decide. When we go to sleep, we go more completely into the subconscious, and those ideas that we take with us when we go to sleep, especially those that engage our serious attention at the time, are completely turned over, so to speak, during the period of sleep, and examined from all points of view. Sometimes it is necessary to take those ideas into the subconscious a number of times when we go to sleep, as well as to submit the matter to the subconscious many times in the day during the waking state, but if we persevere, the right answer will finally be secured. The whole mind, conscious and subconscious, does possess the power to solve any problem that may come up, or provide the necessary ways and means through which we can carry out or finish anything we have undertaken.

Here, as elsewhere, practice makes perfect. The more you train the subconscious to work with you, the easier it becomes to get the subconscious to respond to your directions, and therefore the subconscious mind should be called into action, no matter what comes up; in other words make it a practice to use your whole mind, conscious and subconscious, at all times, not only in large matters, but in all matters. Begin by recognizing the subconscious in all thought and in all action. Think that it can do what you have been told it can do, and eliminate doubt absolutely. Take several moments every day and suggest to the subconscious what you want to have done. Be thoroughly sincere in this matter; be determined; have unbounded faith, and you can expect results; but do not permit the mind to become wrought up when giving directions.

Always be calm and deeply poised when thinking out or suggesting to the subconscious, and it is especially important that you be deeply calm before you go to sleep. Do not permit any idea, suggestion or expectation to enter the subconscious unless it is something that you actually want developed or worked out, and here we should remember that every idea, desire or state of mind that is deeply felt will enter the subconscious. When there are no results, do not lose faith. You know that the cause of the failure was the failure of the conscious to properly touch the subconscious at the time the directions were given, so therefore try again, giving your thought a deeper life and a more persistent desire. Always be prepared to give these methods sufficient time. Some have remarkable results at once, while others secure no results for months; but whether you secure results as soon as you wish or not, continue to give your directions every day, fully expecting results. Be determined in every effort you may make in this direction, but do not be over-anxious. Make it a point to give special directions to the subconscious every day for the steady improvement of mind, character and personality along all lines. You cannot give the subconscious too much to do because its power is immense, and as far as we know, its capacity limitless. Every effort you may make to direct or train the subconscious, will bring its natural results in due time, provided you are always calm, well balanced, persistent, deeply poised and harmonious in all your thoughts and actions.

THE PATH TO GREATER THINGS

Dream constantly of the ideal; work ceaselessly to perfect the real.

Believe in yourself; believe in everybody; believe in all that has existence.

Give the body added strength; give the mind added brilliancy; give the soul added inspiration.

Do your best under every circumstance, and believe that every circumstance will give its best to you.

Live for the realization of more life and for the more efficient use of everything that proceeds from life.

Desire eternally what you want; and act always as if every expectation were coming true.

VI

THE POWER OF SUBJECTIVE THOUGHT

THE first important factor to consider in connection with the study of thought is that every thought does not possess power. In modern times, when thinking has been studied so closely, a great many have come to the conclusion that every thought is itself a force and that it invariably produces certain definite results ; but this is not true, and it is well, for if every thought had power we could not last very long as the larger part of ordinary human thinking is chaotic and destructive.

When we proceed to determine what kinds of thought have power and what kinds have not, we find two distinct forms. The one we call objective, the other subjective. Objective thought is the result of general thinking, such as reasoning, intellectual research, analysis, study, the process of recollection, mind-picturing where there is no feeling, and the usual activities of the intellect. In brief, any mental process that calls forth only the activities of the intellect is objective, and such thinking does not affect the conditions of mind and body to any extent; that is, it does not produce direct results corresponding to its own nature upon the system. It does not immediately affect your health, your happiness, your physical condition nor your mental condition. It may, however, affect these things in the long run, and for that reason must not be ignored.

Subjective thinking is any form of thinking or mind-picturing that has depth of feeling, that goes beneath the surface in its action, that moves through the undercurrents, that acts in and through the psychological field. Subjective thought is synonymous with the thought of the heart, and it is subjective thought that is referred to in the statement, "As a man thinks in his heart so is he." Subjective thought proceeds from the very heart of mental existence; that is, it is always in contact with everything that is vital in life. It is always alive with feeling, and originates, so to speak, in the heart of the mind. The term "heart" in this connection has nothing to do with the physical organ by that name. The term "heart" is here used in its metaphysical sense. We speak of the heart of a great city, meaning thereby, the principal part of the city, or that part of the city where its most vital activities are taking place; likewise, the heart of the mind is the most vital realm of the mind, or the centre of the mind, or the deeper activities of the mind as distinguished from the surface of the mind.

Subjective thinking being in the heart of the mind is therefore necessarily the product of the deepest mental life, and for this reason every subjective thought is a force. It will either work for you or against you, and has the power to produce direct effects upon mind or body, corresponding exactly with its own nature. But all thinking is liable to become subjective at times. All thoughts may sink into the deeper or vital realms of mind and thus become direct forces for good or ill. Therefore, all thinking should be scientific; that is, designed or produced with a definite object in view. All thought should be produced according to the laws of right thinking or constructive thinking. Though objective thinking usually produces no results whatever, nevertheless there are many objective thoughts that become subjective and it is the objective mind that invariably determines the nature of subjective thinking. Every thought therefore should have the right tendency, so that it may produce desirable results in case it becomes subjective, or may act in harmony with the objective mind whenever it is being employed in giving directions to the subjective.

In this connection, it is well to remember that subjective thinking invariably takes place in the subconscious mind, as the terms subjective and subconscious mean practically the same; though in speaking of thought, the term subjective is more appropriate in defining that form of thought that is deep, vital and alive, or that acts through the mental undercurrents.

To define scientific thinking, it may be stated that your thinking is scientific when your thought has a direct tendency to produce what you want, or when all the forces of your mind are working together for the purpose you desire to fulfil. Your thinking is unscientific when your thought has a tendency to produce what is detrimental, or when your mental forces are working against you.

To think scientifically, the first essential is to think only such thoughts and permit only such mental attitudes as you know to be in your favour; and the second essential is to make only such thoughts subjective. In other words, every thought should be right and every thought should be a force. When every thought is scientific, it will be right, and when every thought is subjective it will be a force. Positively refuse to think of what you do not wish to retain or experience. Think only of what you desire, and expect only what you desire, even when the very contrary seems to be coming into your life. Make it a point to have definite results in mind at all times. Permit no thinking to be aimless. Every aimless thought is time and energy wasted, while every thought that is inspired with a definite aim will help to realize that aim, and if all your thoughts are inspired with a definite aim, the whole power of your mind will be for you and will work with you in realizing what you have in view. That you should succeed is therefore assured, because there is enough power in your mind to realize your ambitions, provided all of that power is used in working for your ambitions. And in scientific thinking all the power of mind and thought is being caused to work directly and constantly for what you wish to attain and achieve.

To explain further the nature of scientific thinking, as well as unscientific thinking, it is well to take several well-known illustrations from real life. When things go wrong, people usually say, "That's always the way"; and though this may seem to be a harmless expression, nevertheless, the more you use that expression the more deeply you convince your mind that things naturally go wrong most of the time. When you train your mind to think that it is usual for things to go wrong, the forces of your mind will follow that trend of thinking, and will also go wrong; and for that reason it is perfectly natural that things in your life should go wrong more and more, because as the forces of your mind are going wrong, you will go wrong, and when you go wrong, those things that pertain to your life cannot possibly go right.

A great many people are constantly looking for the worst. They usually expect the worst to happen; though they may be cheerful on the surface, deep down in their heart they are constantly looking for trouble. The result is that their deeper mental currents will tend to produce trouble. If you are always looking for the worst, the forces of your mind will be turned in that direction, and therefore will become destructive. Those forces will tend to produce the very thing that you expect. At first they will simply confuse your mind and produce troubled conditions in your mental world; but this will in turn confuse your faculties, your reason and your judgment, so that you will make many mistakes; and he who is constantly making mistakes will certainly find the worst on many or all occasions.

When things go wrong, do not expect the wrong to appear again. Look upon it as an exception. Call it past and forget it. To be scientific under these circumstances, always look for the best. By constantly expecting the best, you will turn the different forces of your mind and thought to work for the best. Every power that is in you will have a higher and finer ideal upon which to turn its attention, and accordingly, results will be better, which is perfectly natural when your whole system is moving towards the better. A number of people have a habit of saying, "Something is always wrong"; but why should we not say instead, "Something is always right"? We would thereby express more of the truth and give our minds a more wholesome tendency. It is not true that something is always wrong. When we compare the wrong with the right, the wrong is always in the minority. However, it is the effect of such thinking upon the mind that we wish to avoid, whether the wrong be in our midst or not. When you think that there is always something wrong, your mind is more or less concentrated on the wrong, and will therefore create the wrong in your own mentality; but when you train yourself to think there is always something right, your mind will concentrate upon the right, and accordingly will create the right. And when the mind is trained to create the right it will not only produce right conditions within itself, but all thinking will tend to become right; and right thinking invariably leads to health, happiness, power and plenty.

The average person is in the habit of saying, "The older I get"; and they thereby call the attention of the mind to the idea that they are getting older. In brief, they compel their mind to believe that they are getting older and older, and thereby direct the mind to produce more and more age. The true expression in this connection is, "The longer I live." This expression calls the mind's attention to the length of life, which will, in turn, tend to increase the power of that process in you that can prolong life. When people reach the age of sixty or seventy, they usually speak of "the rest of my days," thus implying the idea that there are only a few more days remaining. The mind is thereby directed to finish life in a short period of time, and accordingly, all the forces of the mind will proceed to work for the speedy termination of personal existence. The correct expression is "from now on," as that leads thought into the future indefinitely without impressing the mind with any end whatever.

We frequently hear the expression, "I can never do anything right," and it is quite simple to understand that such a mode of thought would train the mind to act below its true ability and capacity. If you are fully convinced that you can never do anything right, it will become practically impossible for you to do anything right at any time, but on the other hand, if you continue to think, "I am going to do everything better and better," it is quite natural that your entire mental system should be inspired and trained to do things better and better. Hundreds of similar expressions could be mentioned, but we are all familiar with them, and from the comments made above, anyone will realize that such expressions are obstacles in our way, no matter what we may do.

In right thinking the purpose should be never to use any expression that conveys to your mind what you do not want, or what is detrimental or unwholesome in any manner whatever. Think only what you wish to produce or realize. If trouble is brewing, think about the greater success that you have in mind. If anything adverse is about to take place, do not think of what that adversity may bring, but think of the greater good that you are determined to realize in your life. When trouble is brewing, the average person usually thinks of nothing else. Their mind is filled with fear, and not a single faculty in their possession can do justice to itself. And as trouble is usually brewing in most places, more or less, people have what may be called a chronic expectation for trouble; and as they usually get more or less of what they expect, they imagine they are fully justified in entertaining such expectations. But here it is absolutely necessary to change the mind completely. Whatever our present circumstances may be, we should refuse absolutely to expect anything but the best that we can think of. The whole mind, with all its powers and faculties, should be thrown, so to speak, into line with the optimistic tendency, and whatever comes or not, we should think only of the greater things that we expect to realize. In brief, we should concentrate the mind absolutely upon whatever goal we may have in view, and I should look neither to the left nor to the right.

When we concentrate absolutely upon the greater things we expect to attain or achieve, we gradually train all the forces of the mind and all the powers of thought to work for those greater things. We shall thereby begin in earnest to build for ourselves a greater destiny; and sooner or later we shall find ourselves gaining ground in many directions. Later on, if we proceed, we shall begin to move more rapidly, and if we pay no attention to the various troubles that may be brewing in our environment, those troubles will never affect us nor disturb us in the least.

The mental law involved in the process of scientific thinking may be stated as follows: The more you think of what is right, the more you tend to make every action in your mind right. The more you think of the goal you have in view, the more life and power you will call into action in working for that goal. The more you think of your ambition, the more power you will give to those faculties that can make your ambitions come true. The more you think of harmony, of health, of success, of happiness, of things that are desirable, of things that are beautiful, of things that have true worth, the more the mind will tend to build all those things in yourself, provided, of course, that all such thinking is subjective.

To think scientifically, therefore, is to train your every thought and your every mental action to focus the whole of attention upon that which you wish to realize, to gain, to achieve or attain in your life.

In training the mind along the lines of scientific thinking begin by trying to hold the mind upon the right, regardless of the presence of the wrong, and here we should remember that the term "right" does not simply refer to moral actions, but to all actions. When the wrong is com ing your way, persist in thinking of the right; persist in expecting only the right. And there is a scientific reason for this attitude, besides what has been mentioned above. We know that the most important of all is to keep the mind right or moving along right lines, and if we persistently expect the right, regardless of circumstances, the mind will be kept in the lines of right action. But there is another result that frequently comes from this same practice. It sometimes happens that the wrong which is brewing in your environment, has such a weak foundation that only a slight increase in the force of the right would be necessary to overthrow that wrong completely; in fact, we shall find that most wrongs that threaten can be overcome in a very short time, if we continue to work for the right in a positive, constructive, determined manner. It is when the individual goes all to pieces, so to speak, that adversity gets the best of them; but no individual will go to pieces unless their thinking is chaotic, destructive, scattered, confused and detrimental. Continue to possess your whole mind and you will master the situation, no matter what it may be, and it is scientific thinking that will enable you to perform this great feat.

To make thinking scientific, there are three leading essentials to be observed. The first is to cultivate constructive mental attitudes, and all mental attitudes are constructive when mind, thought, feeling, desire and will constantly face the greater and the better. A positive and determined optimism has the same effect, and the same is true of the practice of keeping the mental eye single on the highest goal in view. To make every mental attitude constructive the mind must never look down, and mental depression must be avoided completely. Every thought and every feeling must have an upward look, and every desire must desire to inspire the same rising tendency in every action of mind.

The second essential is constructive mental imagery. Use the imagination to picture only what is good, what is beautiful, what is beneficial, what is ideal, and what you wish to realize. Mentally see yourself receiving what you deeply desire to receive. What you imagine, you will think, and what you think, you will become. Therefore, if you imagine only those things that are in harmony with what you wish to obtain or achieve, all your thinking will soon tend to produce what you want to attain or achieve.

The third essential is constructive mental action. Every action of the mind should have something desirable in view and should have a definite, positive aim. Train yourself to face the sunshine of life regardless of circumstances. When you face the sunshine, everything looks right, and when everything looks right, you will think right. It matters not whether there is any sunshine in life just now or not. We must think of sunshine just the same. If we do not see any silver lining, we must create one in our own mental vision. However dark the dark side may seem to be, we cannot afford to see anything but the bright side, and no matter how small or insignificant the bright side may be, we must continue to focus attention on that side alone. Be optimistic, not in the usual sense of that term, but in the real sense of that term. The true optimist not only expects the best to happen, but goes to work to make the best happen. The true optimist not only looks upon the bright side, but trains every force that is in them to produce more and more brightness in their life, and therefore complies with the three essentials just mentioned. Their mental attitudes are constructive because they are always facing greater things. Their imagination is constructive because it is always picturing the better and the ideal, and their mental actions are constructive because they are training the whole of their life to produce those greater and better things that their optimism has inspired them to desire and expect.

In this connection, we must remember that there is a group of mental forces at work in every mental attitude, and therefore if that attitude is downcast, those forces will become detrimental; that is, they will work for the lesser and the inferior. On the other hand, if every mental attitude is lifted up or directed towards the heights of the great and the true and the ideal, those forces will become constructive, and will work for the greater things in view.

In the perusal of this study, we shall find it profitable to examine our mental attitudes closely, so as to determine what our minds are actually facing the greater part of the time. If we find that we are mentally facing things and conditions that are beneath our expectations, or find that our imaginations are concerned too much about possible failure, possible mistakes, possible trouble, possible adversity, etc., our thinking is unscientific, and no time should be lost in making amends.

When you are looking into the future, do not worry about troubles that might come to pass. Do not mentally see yourself as having a hard time of it. Do not imagine yourself in this hostile condition or that adverse circumstance. Do not wonder what you would do if you should lose everything, or if this or that calamity should befall. Such thinking is decidedly unscientific and most detrimental. If you entertain such thoughts you are causing the ship of your life to move directly towards the worst precipice that may exist in your vicinity. Besides, you are so weakening this ship through wrong treatment, that it will some day spring a leak and go down.

Think of the future whenever it is unnecessary for you to give your attention to the present, but let your thought of the future be wholesome, constructive, optimistic and ideal. Mentally see yourself gaining the best that life has to give, and you will meet more and more of the best. Think of yourself as gaining ground along all lines, as finding better and better circumstances, as increasing in power and ability, and as becoming more healthful in body, more vigorous and brilliant in mind, more perfect in character, and more powerful in soul. In brief, associate your future with the best that you can think of along all lines. Fear nothing for the days that are to be, but expect everything that is good, desirable, enjoyable and ideal. This practice will not only make your present happier, but it will tend to strengthen your mind and your life along wholesome constructive lines to such a degree that you will actually gain the power to realize, in a large measure, those beautiful and greater things that you have constantly expected in your optimistic dreams.

In living and building for a larger future, we should remember that our mind and thoughts invariably follow the leadership of the most prominent mental picture. The man who clearly and distinctly pictures for himself a brilliant future will inspire the powers of his entire mental world to work for such a future; in fact, all the forces of thought, mind, life, personality, character and soul will move in that direction. He may not realize as brilliant a future as he has pictured, but his future is certainly going to be brilliant, and it is quite possible, as is frequently the case, that it may become even more brilliant than he dreamed of in the beginning.

When the average mind thinks of the future, he usually picture a variety of conflicting events and conditions. He has nothing definite in mind. There is no actual leadership therefore in his mind, and nothing of great worth can be accomplished.

When we look into the lives of men and women who have reached high places, we always find that they were inspired with some great idea. That idea was pictured again and again in their mental vision, and they refused to let it go. They clung tenaciously to that idea, and thereby actually compelled every force and element within them to enlist in the working out of that idea. It is therefore simple enough that they should realize every aim and reach the highest places that achievement has in store. Such men and women possibly did not understand the science or the process, but they were nevertheless thinking scientifically to a most perfect degree. Their ambition pictured only that lofty goal which they wanted to reach. All their mental attitudes were constantly facing that lofty goal, and thereby became constructive; and all the actions of mind were directed toward the same goal. Accordingly, everything within them was trained to work for the realization of their dream, and that is what we mean by scientific thinking; that is what we mean by thinking for results. And anyone who will train themselves to think for results in this manner, will positively secure results; though in this connection it is well to remember that persistence and determination are indispensable every step of the way.

When we do not secure results at once, we sometimes become discouraged, and conclude that it is no use to try. At such times, friends will usually tell us that we are simply dreaming, and they will advise us to go to work at something practical, something that we really can accomplish; but if we ignore the advice of our friends, and continue to be true to the great idea that we have resolved to work out, we shall finally reach our goal, and when we do, those very same friends will tell us that we took the proper course. So long as the man with ambition is a failure, the world will tell him to let go of his ideal; but when his ambition is realized, the world will praise him for the persistence and the determination that he manifested during his dark hours, and everybody will point to his life as an example for coming generations. This is invariably the rule. Therefore pay no attention to what the world says when you are down. Be determined to get up, to reach the highest goal you have in view, and you will.

There are a great many ambitious men and women, who imagine that they will succeed provided their determination is strong and their persistence continuous, regardless of the fact that their thinking may be unscientific; but the sooner we dispel this illusion, the better. Unscientific thinking, even in minor matters, weakens the will. It turns valuable thought power astray, and we need the full power of thought, positively directed along the line of our work if we are going to achieve, and achieve greatly.

The majority of the mental forces in the average person are working against them, because they are constantly entertaining depressed mental states or detrimental habits of thought; and even though they may be ambitious, that ambition has not sufficient power to work itself out, because most of the forces of their mind are thrown away. We therefore see the necessity of becoming scientific in all thinking, and in making every mental habit wholesome and beneficial in the largest sense of those terms. But scientific thinking not only tends to turn the power of thought in the right direction; it also tends to increase mental power, to promote efficiency and to build up every faculty that we may employ.

To illustrate the effect of right thinking upon the faculties, we will suppose that you have musical talent, and are trying to perfect that talent. Then, we will suppose that you are constantly expressing dissatisfaction with the power of that talent. What will be the result? Your mental action upon that faculty will tend to lower its efficiency, because you are depressing its action instead of inspiring those actions. On the other hand, if you encourage this talent, you will tend to expand its life, and thereby increase its capacity for results.

In this respect, talents are similar to people. Take two people of equal ability and place them in circumstances that are direct opposites. We will suppose that the one is mistreated every day by those with whom he is associated. He is constantly being criticized and constantly being told that he will never amount to anything; he is blamed for everything that is wrong, and is in every manner discouraged and kept down. What would happen to the ability and efficiency of that man if he continued under such treatment year after year? He simply could not advance unless he should happen to be a mental giant, and even then, his advancement would be very slow; but if he was not a mental giant, just an average man, he would steadily lose ambition, self-confidence, initiative, judgment, reasoning power, and in fact, everything that goes to make up ability and capacity.

We will suppose the other man is encouraged continually. He is praised for every thing, he is given every possible opportunity to show and apply what ability he may possess; he is surrounded by an optimistic atmosphere, and is expected by everybody to advance and improve continually. What will happen to this man? The best will be brought out in his power and ability. He will be pushed to the fore constantly and he will climb steadily and surely until he reaches the top.

Treat your talents in the same way, and you have the same results in every case. To state it briefly, make it a point to encourage your talents, your faculties and your powers. Give every element and force within you encouragement and inspiration. Expect them all to do their best, and train yourself to think and feel that they positively will. Train yourself to think of your whole system as all right. Deal with your mental faculties in this manner, under all circumstances, and deal with your physical organs in the same way.

Most people among those who do not have perfect health, have a habit of speaking of their stomachs as bad, their livers as always out of order, their eyes as weak, their nerves as all upset, and the different parts of their systems as generally wrong. But what are they doing to their physical organs through this practice? The very same as was done to the unfortunate man just mentioned, and we shall find, in this connection, one reason why so many people continue to be sick. They are keeping their physical organs down, so to speak, by depressing the entire system with unwholesome thinking; but if they would change their tactics and begin to encourage their physical organs, praise them and expect them to do better, and to treat them right from the mental as well as a physical standpoint, they would soon be restored to perfect health.

In training the mind in scientific thinking, the larger part of attention should be given to that of controlling our feelings. It is not difficult to think scientifically along intellectual lines, but to make our feelings move along wholesome, constructive, optimistic lines requires persistent training. Intellectual thought can be changed almost at anytime with little effort, but feeling usually becomes stronger and stronger the longer it moves along a certain line, and thus becomes more difficult to change. When we feel discouraged, it is so easy to feel more discouraged; when we feel dissatisfied, it is only a step to that condition that is practically intolerable. It is therefore necessary to stop all detrimental feeling in the beginning. Do not permit a single adverse feeling to continue for a second. Change the mind at once by turning your attention upon something that will make you feel better. Resolve to feel the way you want to feel under all circumstances, and you will gradually develop the power to do so. Depressed mental feelings are burdens, and we waste a great deal of energy by carrying them around on our mental shoulders. Besides, such feelings tend to direct the power of thought towards the lower and the inferior. Whenever you permit yourself to feel bad, you will cause the power of mind and thought to go wrong. Therefore, persist in feeling right and good. Persist in feeling joyous. Persist in feeling cheerful, hopeful, optimistic and strong. Place yourself on the bright side and the strong side of everything that transpires in your life, and you will constantly gain power, power that will invariably be in your favour.

Life is growth and the object of right thinking is to promote that growth.

Give less time trying to change the opinions of others, and more time trying to improve your own life.

Life becomes the way it is lived; and man may live the way he wants to live when he learns to think what he wants to think.

Create your own thought and you become what you want to become because your thought creates you.

We all know that man is as he thinks. Then we must think only such thoughts as tend to make us what we wish to be.

The secret of right thinking is found in always keeping the mind's eye stayed upon the greater and the better in all things.

CLOSED EYES

VII
HOW MAN BECOMES WHAT HE THINKS

SCIENTIFIC research in the metaphysical field has demonstrated the fact that man is as he thinks, that he becomes what he thinks, and that what he thinks in the present, determines what he is to become in the future; and also that since he can change his thought for the better along any line, he can therefore completely change himself along any line. But the majority who try to apply this law do not succeed to a great degree, the reason being that instead of working entirely upon the principle that man is as he thinks, they proceed in the belief that man is what he thinks he is.

At first sight there may seem to be no difference between the principle that man is as he thinks and the belief that man is as he thinks he is, but close study will reveal the fact that the latter is absolutely untrue. Man is not what he thinks he is, because personality, mentality and character are not determined by personal opinions. It is the thought of the heart, that is, the mental expression from the subconscious that makes the personal man what he is; but the subconscious is effected only by what man actually thinks in the real field of creative thought, and not by what he may think of himself in the field of mere personal opinion.

It is subjective thought that makes you what you are; but to think that you are thus or so, will not necessarily make you thus or so. To create subjective thought you must act directly upon the subconscious, but it is not possible to impress the subconscious while you are forming opinions about your personal self. A mere statement about yourself will not affect or change the subconscious, and so long as the subconscious remains unchanged, you will remain unchanged. While you are thinking simply about your external or personal self you are acting upon the objective, but to change yourself you must act upon the subjective.

Man may think that he is great, but so long as he continues to think small thoughts, he will continue to be small. No matter how high an opinion he may have of himself, while he is living in the superficial, his thoughts will be empty, and empty thoughts are not conducive to high attainments and great achievements. Man becomes great when he thinks great thoughts, and to think great thoughts he must transcend the limitations and circumscribed conditions of the person, and mentally enter into the world of the great and the superior. He must seek to gain a larger and a larger consciousness of the world of real quality, real worth and real superiority, and must dwell upon the loftiest mountain peaks of mind that be can possibly reach. He must live in the life of greatness, breathe the spirit of greatness, and feel the very soul of greatness. Then, and only then, will he think great thoughts; and the mind that continues to think great thoughts will continue to grow in greatness.

It is not what you state in your thought but what you give to your thought that determines results. The thought that is merely stated may be empty, but it is the thought with something in it that alone can exercise real power in personal life. And what is to be in your thought will depend upon what you think into your thought. What you give to your thought, your thought will give to you, and you will be and become accordingly, no matter what you may think that you are. The cause that you originate in the within will produce its effect in the without, regardless of what your opinions may be. Your personal life will consequently be the result of what you think, but it will not necessarily be what you think it is.

Having discovered the fact that the physical body is completely renewed every eight or ten months, you will naturally think that you are young, but to simply think you are young will not cause the body to look as young as it really is. To retain your youth you must remove those subconscious tendencies and conditions that produce old age, and you must eliminate worry. So long as you worry you will cause your personality to grow older and older in appearance, no matter how persistently you may think that you are young. To simply think that you are young will not avail. You must think thoughts that produce, retain and perpetuate youth. If you wish to look young, your mind must feel young, but you will not feel young until the whole of your mind produces the feeling of youth.

To develop the feeling of youth in the whole mind, you must become fully conscious of the fact that youth is naturally produced in your entire system every minute, and you must train the mind to take cognizance only of the eternal now. So long as we feel that we are passing with time, we will imagine that we feel the weight of more and more years, and this feeling will invariably cause the body to show the mark of years, growing older and older in appearance as more years are added to the imaginary burden of age. You will look young when you feel young, but to simply feel that you are young will not always cause you to feel young. The real feeling of youth comes when we actually think in the consciousness of youth and give the realization of the now to every thought.

You may think that you are well, but you will not secure health until you think thoughts that produce health. You may persistently affirm that you are well, but so long as you live in discord, confusion, worry, fear and other wrong states of mind, you will be sick; that is, you will be as you think and not what you think you are. You may state health in your thought, but if you give worry, fear and discord to that thought, your thinking will produce discord. It is not what we state in our thoughts, but what we give to our thoughts that determine results. To produce health, thought itself must be healthful and wholesome. It must contain the quality of health, and the very life of health. This, however, is not possible unless the mind is conscious of health at the time when such thought is being produced. Therefore, to think thoughts that can produce health, the mind must enter into the realization of the being of health, and not simply dwell in the objective belief about health. Again, to produce health, all the laws of life must be observed; that is, the mind must be in that understanding of law, and in that harmony with law where the guiding thought will naturally observe law. To simply think that you are well will not teach the mind to understand the laws of life and health, nor will that thinking place you in harmony with those laws. That thinking that does understand the laws of life will not come from the mere belief that you are well, but from the effort to enter into the understanding of all law, the spirit of all law, the very life of health, and into the very soul of all truth.

You may think that your mind is brilliant and may undertake most difficult tasks in the belief that you are equal to the occasion, but the question is if your conception of brilliancy is great or small. If your conception of brilliancy is small, you may be right to that degree in thinking you are brilliant; that is, you may be brilliant as far as your understanding of brilliancy goes. Whether that is sufficient or not to carry out the task that is before you is another question. Your opinion of your mental capacity may be great, but if your idea of intelligence is crude, your intelligence- producing thought will also be crude, and can produce only crude intelligence. It is therefore evident that to simply think that you are brilliant will not produce brilliancy, unless your understanding of brilliancy is made larger, higher and finer. What you understand and mentally feel concerning intelligence mental capacity and brilliancy, is what you actually think on those subjects, and it is this understanding or feeling or realization that will determine how much intelligence you will give to your thought. Your thought will be as brilliant as the brilliancy you think into your thought, and how much brilliancy you will think into your thought will depend upon how high your realization of brilliancy happens to be at the time. When your thinking is brilliant, you will be brilliant, but if your thinking is not brilliant you will not be brilliant, no matter how brilliant you may think you are.

To make your thinking more brilliant, try to enter into the consciousness of finer intelligence, larger mental capacity, and the highest order of mental brilliancy that you can possibly realize. Do not call yourself brilliant at any time, or do not think of yourself as lacking in brilliancy. Simply fix the mental eye upon absolute brilliancy, and desire with all the power of mind and soul to go on and on into higher steps of that brilliancy.

When all the elements and forces of your system are working in such a way that beauty will naturally be produced, you will be beautiful, whether you think you are beautiful or not, and it is the actions of the subconscious that determine how the elements and forces of the system are to work. Therefore, the beautiful person is beautiful because her real interior thinking is conducive to the creation of the beautiful. That person, however, who is not beautiful, does not necessarily think ugly thoughts, but her interior mental actions have not been brought together in such a way as to produce the expression of beauty; that is the subconscious actions have not been arranged according to the most perfect pattern. But these actions can be arranged in that manner, not by thinking that one is beautiful. but by thinking thoughts that are beautiful.

When you think that you are beautiful, you are liable to think that you are more beautiful than others, and such a thought is not a beautiful thought. To recognize or criticize ugliness and inferiority in others is to create the inferior and the ugly in yourself, and what you create in yourself will sooner or later be expressed through your mind and personality. So long as you worry, hate or fear, your thought will make you disagreeable in mind and character, and later on in the person as well; and no amount of affirming or thinking that you are beautiful will overcome those ugly states of mind that you have created. You will thus be as you think—worried, hateful and ugly, and not beautiful as you may try to think you are.

The personal man is the result, not of beliefs or opinions, but of the quality of all the mental actions that are at work throughout the whole mind. Man is as he thinks in every thought, and not what he thinks he is in one or more isolated parts of his personal self. You may think that you are good, but your idea of goodness may be wrong. Your thought therefore will not be conducive to goodness. On the contrary, the more you praise yourself for being good, the less goodness you will express in your nature. In addition, to think of yourself as good will have a tendency to produce a feeling of self-righteousness. This feeling will cause the mind to look down upon the less fortunate, and a mind that looks down will soon begin to go down, and you will be no better than those whom you criticized before. You are only as good as the sum total of all your good thoughts, and these can be increased in number indefinitely by training the mind to perpetually grow in the consciousness of absolute goodness.

To grow in the consciousness of goodness, keep the mental eye upon the highest conception of absolute goodness. Try to enlarge, elevate and define this conception or understanding of goodness perpetually. Pattern your whole life, all your thoughts and all your actions after the likeness of this highest understanding. Then never look back nor try to measure the goodness that you may think you now possess. Press on eternally to the higher and larger realization of absolute goodness, and leave results to the law. More and more real goodness will naturally appear in all your thoughts and actions. You will therefore become good, not by thinking that you are good, but by thinking thoughts that are created in the image and likeness of that which is good.

From the foregoing it is evident that man is as he thinks, and not necessarily what he thinks he is. But there is still more evidence. That your personal self is the result of your thought has been demonstrated, but what thought? To make yourself thus or so, the necessary thought must first be created but to think that you are thus or so, will not create the thought that can make you thus or so. The reason is because it is subconscious thought alone that can produce effects in your nature, physical or mental, and you cannot enter the subconscious while you are thinking exclusively of your personal self. What you think about yourself is always objective thought, and mere objective thought is powerless to effect or change anything in your nature. To think thoughts that can give you more life, you must enter into the consciousness of absolute life, but you cannot enter the absolute while you are defining or measuring the personal. If you wish to possess more quality, you must give your thoughts more quality and worth, you must forget the lesser worth of the personal and enter into the consciousness of the greater worth of absolute worth itself.

So long as you think that you are thus or so in the personal sense, your thought will be on the surface. You will mentally live among effects. You will not create new causes, therefore will not produce any changes in yourself. You will continue to be as you are thinking deep down in the subconscious where hereditary tendencies, habits, race thoughts and other mental forces continue their usual work, regardless of your personal opinion or empty thoughts on the surface.

To change yourself you must go to that depth of mind where the causes of your personal condition exist. But your mind will not enter the depth of the within so long as your thought is on the surface and your thought will be on the surface so long as you are thinking exclusively about your personal self. The secret therefore is not to form opinions about yourself or to think about yourself as being thus or so, but to form larger conceptions of principles and qualities. Enter the richness of real life and you will think richer thoughts. Forget the limitations, the weaknesses and the shortcomings of your personal self as well as your superficial opinions of your personal self, and enter mentally into the greatness, the grandeur, the sublimity and the splendour of all things. Seek to gain a larger and a larger understanding of the majesty and marvellousness of all life, and aspire to think the thoughts of the Infinite.

This is the secret of thinking great thoughts, and he will positively become great whose thoughts are always great. In like manner, he who thinks wholesome thoughts, and wholesome thoughts only, will become healthful and wholesome. Such thoughts will have the power to produce health, and thoughts never fail to do what they have the power to do. Place in action the necessary subconscious thought and the expected results will invariably follow.

Man therefore is not what he thinks he is because such thinking is personal and consequently superficial and powerless. The thought that determines his personality, his character, his mentality and his destiny is his subjective thought the thought that is produced in the subconscious during those moments when he forgets his personal opinions about himself and permits his mind to act with deep feeling and subjective conviction. But those thoughts that enter the subconscious are not always good thoughts. Man's subjective thinking is not always conducive to the true, the wholesome and the best, as his thinking is not always right. For this reason, man himself is not always good, nor his life as beautiful as he might wish to be. His thinking is in his own hands, however. He can learn to think what he wants to think, and as he is and becomes as he thinks, we naturally conclude that he may, in the course of time, become what he wants to become.

The greatest remedy in the world is change; and change implies the passing from the old to the new. It is also the only path that leads from the lesser to the greater, from the dream to the reality, from the wish to the heart's desire fulfilled. It is change that brings us everything we want. It is the opposite of change that holds us back from that which we want. But change is not always external. Real change, or rather the cause of all change, is always internal. It is the change in the within that first produces the change in the without. To go from place to place is not a change unless it produces a change of mind a renewal of mind. It is the change of mind that is the change desired. It is the renewal of mind that produces better health, more happiness, greater power, the increase of life, and the consequent increase of all that is good in life. And the constant renewal of mind—the daily change of mind—is possible regardless of times, circumstances or places. He who can change his mind every day and think the new about everything every day, will always be well; he will always have happiness; he will always be free; his life will always be interesting; he will constantly move forward into the larger, the richer and the better; and whatever is needed for his welfare today, of that he shall surely have abundance.

Light

VIII
THE ART OF CHANGING FOR THE BETTER

PERSONAL man gradually but surely grows into the likeness of that which he thinks of the most, and man thinks the most of what he loves the best. This is the law through which man has become what he is, and it is through the intelligent use of this law that man may change for the better and improve in any way desired. The thought you think not only effects your character, your mind and your body, but also produces the original cause of every characteristic, every habit, every tendency, every desire, every mental quality and every physical condition that appears in your system. Thought is the one original cause of the conditions, characteristics and peculiarities of the human personality, and everything that appears in the personality is the direct or indirect effect of the various actions of thought. It is therefore evident that man naturally grows into the likeness of the thought he thinks, and it is also evident that the nature of his thought would be determined by that which he thinks of the most.

The understanding of this fact will reveal to all minds the basic law of change, and though it is basic, its intelligent use may become simplicity itself. Through the indiscriminate use of this law, man has constantly been changing, sometimes for the better, sometimes not, but by the conscious, intelligent, use of this law he may change only for the better and as rapidly as the sum total of his present ability will permit.

The fact that mental conditions and dispositions may be changed through the power of thought, will readily be accepted by every mind, but that mental qualities, abilities, personal appearances and physical conditions may be changed in the same way all minds may not be ready to accept. Nevertheless, that thought can change anything in the human system, even to a remarkable degree, is now a demonstrated fact. We have all seen faces change for the worse under the influence of grief, worry and misfortune, and we have observed that all people grow old who expect to do so, regardless of the fact that the body of the octogenarian is not a day older than the body of a little child. We have unlimited evidence to prove that ability will improve or deteriorate according to the use that is made of the mind. A man's face reveals his thought, and we can invariably detect the predominating states of the mind that lives in a groove. When a person changes their mental states at frequent intervals, no one state has the opportunity to produce an individual, clear-cut expression, and therefore cannot be so readily detected, but where one predominating state is continued in action for weeks or months or years, anyone can say what that state is, by looking at the face of the one who has it. Thus we can detect different kinds of disposition, different grades of mind, different degrees of character and different modes of living, and convince ourselves at the same time, that man in general, looks, acts and lives the way he thinks.

The fact that every mental state will express its nature in body, mind and character, proves that we can, through the intelligent use of mental action, cause the body to become more beautiful, the mind more brilliant, character more powerful and the soul life more ideal. To accomplish these things, however, it is necessary to apply the law continuously in that direction where we desire to secure results. When a person thinks of the ordinary for a few weeks, they invariably begin to look ordinary. Then when something impels them to think for a while of the ideal, the true and the beautiful, they begin to look like a new creature; but if reverses threaten, they will feel worried, dejected and afraid, and everybody observes that they look bad. Then if the tide turns in their favour, they will begin to look content, and if something should suggest to their mind the thought of the wholesome, the sound and the harmonious, they will begin to look remarkably well. In this manner they are daily using the law of change, but never intelligently. They do not take the law into their own hands, but use the law only as suggestions from their environment may direct. They advance one day and fall back the next. One week their physical mansion is painted with colours of health and beauty; the next week only the conditions of age and disease are in evidence. They plant a flower seed today, and tomorrow they hoe it up to plant a weed in its place. Thus the average person continues to live, and every change comes from the unconscious, indiscriminate use of the power of their thought. This power, however, can be employed more wisely, and when the many begin to do so, the progress of the race will be remarkable indeed.

The basic law of change must be taken into our own hands, and must be employed directly for producing the change we have in view; and to accomplish this the love nature must be so trained that we shall love only what we want to love, only what is greater and better than that which we have realized up to the present time. In this respect strong, highly developed souls will have no difficulty, because they have the power to see the great, the beautiful and the ideal in all things, but those who have not as yet acquired that power, must train their feelings with care, lest love frequently turns thought upon the low, the common or the ordinary.

What you admire in others will develop in yourself. Therefore, to love the ordinary in anyone is to become ordinary, while to love the noble and the lofty in all minds is to grow into the likeness of that which is noble and lofty. When we love the person of someone who is in the earth earthy, we tend to keep ourselves down in the same place. We may give our kindness and our sympathies to all, but we must not love anything in anyone that is not ideal. It is a misdirection of love to love exclusively the visible person. It is the ideal, the true and the beautiful in every person that should be loved, and as all persons have these qualities, we can love everybody with a whole heart in this more sublime manner.

In this connection a great problem presents itself to many men and women who aspire to a life of great quality. These people feel that they cannot give their personal love to husbands, wives, relatives or friends that persist in living in the mere animal world; but the problem is easily solved. We must not love what is ordinary in anyone; in fact, the ordinary must not be recognized, but we can love the real life in everyone, and if we will employ our finer perceptions we will find that this real life is ideal in every living creature in the world. We need not love the perversions of a person, but we can love the greater possibilities and the superior qualities that are inherent in the individual. It is not the imperfections or appearances that should be loved, but the greatness that is within; and what we love in others we not only awaken in others, but we develop those very things more or less in ourselves.

To promote the best welfare of individuals under all sorts of circumstances, personal loves should be exchanged only by persons who live in the same world. When the woman has found the superior world, the man must not expect her personal love unless he also goes up to live in the same world. It is simply fair that he should do so. The woman who lives in a small world must not expect the love of a man who lives in a great world. He would lose much of his greatness if he should give his personal love to such a woman.

The tendency of all life is onward and upward. Therefore, to ask anything to come down is to violate the very purpose of existence. If we wish to be with the higher, the greater and the superior, we must change ourselves and become higher, greater and superior; and this we all can do.

In the application of the basic law of change, no factor is more important than that of pleasure. We are controlled to a great extent by the pleasures we enjoy, ofttimes so much so that they may even determine our destiny. The reason why is found in the fact that we deeply love what we thoroughly enjoy, and since we think the most of what we love the best, we naturally become like the pleasures we thoroughly enjoy, because man gradually grows into the likeness of his predominating thought. It is therefore unwise to permit ourselves to enjoy anything that is beneath our most perfect conception of the ideal, and it is likewise unwise to associate personally with people who care only for the ordinary and the common. What we enjoy becomes a part of ourselves, and for the good of everybody, we cannot afford to go down; but when we love only those pleasures that are as high as our own ideal of joy, then we are truly on the great ascending path.

To overlook the wrongs, the defects and the perversions of life, and to look only for that beautiful something in every soul that we simply want to love, even without trying, is one of the greatest things that we can do; but we must not permit our conception of the beautiful within to become a mere, cold abstraction. It is most important that we be as emotional as we possibly can without permitting ourselves to be controlled by our emotions. The heart should be most tender and warm, and every feeling constantly on fire; but if all such feelings are turned into the secret realms of soul life, we shall find that the forces of love are drawn insistently towards the highest, the truest, and most noble and the most beautiful that our inspired moments have revealed. When this is done we can readily love with the whole heart any noble quality, or high art, or great work upon which we may direct our attention, and what we can love at will, that we can think of as deeply and as long as we may desire.

When we have formulated in our minds what changes we wish to make, the course to pursue is to love the ideal that corresponds to those changes. This love must be deep and strong, and must be continued until the desired change has actually taken place. Know what better qualities you want; then love those qualities with all your mind and heart and soul.

To love the higher and the greater qualities of life is to cause the creative qualities of mind to produce those same qualities in our own nature; and in consequence, we steadily grow into the likeness of that which we constantly love. This is the great law—the law that governs all change for the better. But to use this law intelligently the power of love must cease to respond to every whim or notion that the suggestibility of environment may present to the mind.

The power of love is the greatest power in the world, but it can cause persons or nations to fall to the lowest state, as well as rise to the highest state. Every fall in the history of the race has been caused largely by the misdirection of love, while every step in advance has been prompted largely by the power of love turned upon better things. To misdirect love is to love that which is beneath our present stage in advancement; it is turning the forces of life backward, and retrogression must inevitably follow.

In the average person, love is directed almost exclusively upon the personal side of life. In consequence, the love nature becomes so personal, so limited and so superficial, that materialism follows. In many other minds, it is mere appearances that attract the power of admiration, and the finer things in mind, soul and character, are wholly ignored. The result is that the finer qualities of such people gradually disappear, and grossness, both in thought and in appearance naturally follow. But we must not conclude in this connection that it is wrong to admire the beautiful wherever it may be seen in the external world. We should love the beautiful everywhere, no matter where it may be found; we should admire the richness of life, both in the external and in the internal; and by living a complete life, we shall enjoy more and more of the richness and the beautiful in life, in the within as well as in the without. But the power of love must direct the greater part of its attention upon that which is rich and beautiful in mind and soul. It is that which is finer than the finest of external things that must be loved if man is to grow into the likeness of the great, the superior and the ideal, because man is as he thinks, and he thinks the most of what he loves the best.

When any individual begins to love the finer qualities in life, and gives all the power of mind and soul to that love, he has taken the first step in the changing of his destiny. He is laying the foundation for a great and a better future, and if he continues as he has begun, he will positively reach the loftiest goal that he may have in view. There are many laws to apply in the beginning of a great life, but the law that lies at the foundation of them all is the law of love. It is love that determines what we are to think, what we are to work for, where we are to go, and what we are to accomplish. Therefore, among all great essentials, the principal one is to know how to love.

To apply this essential for all practical purposes, the secret is to love the great, the beautiful, and the ideal in everybody and in everything; and to love with such a strong, passionate love that its ascending power becomes irresistible. The whole of life will thus change and go up with the power of love into the great, the superior and the ideal; everything, both in the being of man and in his environment will advance and change accordingly, and the dreams of the soul will come true. The ideal will become real, the desires of the heart will be granted, and what man has hoped to make his own will be absent no more.

When failure comes be more determined than ever to succeed.

The more feeling there is in your thought the greater its power.

You steadily and surely become in the real what you constantly and clearly think that you are in the ideal.

The more you believe in yourself the more of your latent powers and possibilities you place in action. And the more you believe in your purpose the more of your power you apply in promoting that purpose.

To him who thinks he can, everything is an opportunity.

Depend only upon yourself but work in harmony with all things. Thus you call forth the best that is in yourself and secure the best that external sources have to give.

IX

HE CAN WHO THINKS HE CAN

THE discovery of the fact that man is as he thinks, has originated a number of strange ideas concerning the power of thought. One of the principal of these is the belief that thought is a domineering force to be used in controlling things and in compelling fate to come our way. But that this belief is unscientific in every sense of the term has been demonstrated any number of times.

Those who have accepted this belief, and who have tried to use thought as a compelling force, have seemingly succeeded in the beginning, but later on have utterly failed, and the reason is that the very moment we proceed to apply thought in this manner, we place ourselves out of harmony with everything, both within ourselves and in our environment. The seeming success that such people have had in the beginning, or for a season, is due to the fact that a strong compelling force can cause the various elements of life to respond for a while, but the force that compels, weakens itself through the very act of compelling, and finally loses its power completely; and then, whatever has been gathered begins to slip away.

This explains why thousands of ardent students of metaphysics have failed to secure the results desired, or have succeeded only in spurts. They have taken the wrong view of the power of thought, and therefore have caused their power to work against them during the greater part of the time. The power of thought is not a compelling force. It is a building force, and it is only when used in the latter sense that desirable results can be produced. The building capacity of thought, however, is practically unlimited. Therefore there is actually no end to what might be accomplished, so long as this power is employed intelligently.

To apply the full building power of thought, we should proceed upon the principle that he can who thinks he can, and we should act in the full conviction that whatever man thinks he can do, he can do, because there is no limit to the power that such thinking can bring forth. The majority among intelligent minds admit that there is some truth in the statement that he can who thinks he can, but they do not, as a rule, believe it to be a very large truth. They admit that we gain more confidence in ourselves when we think that we can do what we have undertaken to do, and also that we become more determined, but aside from that, they see no further value in that particular attitude of mind. They do not realize that he who thinks he can, develops the power that can; but this is the truth, and it is one of the most important of all truths in the vast metaphysical domain.

The law that governs this idea, and its process while in action, is absolutely unlimited in its possibilities, and therefore is in a position to promise almost anything to one who is faithful. When a person begins to think that they can do certain things that they desire to do, their mind will naturally proceed to act on those faculties that are required in the working out of their purpose; and so long as the mind acts upon a certain faculty, more and more life, nourishment and energy will accumulate in that faculty. In consequence, that faculty will steadily develop. It will become larger, stronger and more efficient, until it finally is competent to do what we originally wanted done. Thus we understand how he who thinks he can develops the power that can.

When a man begins to think that they can apply the power of invention, their mind will begin to act upon the faculty of invention. The latent powers of this faculty will be aroused. These powers will accordingly be exercised more and more, and development will be promoted. This, however, is not all. Whenever the mind

53

concentrates its attention upon a certain faculty, additional energy will be drawn into that faculty; thus power will be added to power, much will gather more, and as this may continue indefinitely there need be no end to the capacity and the ability that can be developed in that faculty. In the course of time, be it in a few months or in a few years, that person will actually have developed the power of invention to such a degree that they can invent successfully; and through the application of the same law, can further develop this same faculty, year after year, until they may finally become an inventive genius. When a man has some inventive power in the beginning, they will secure, through the application of this law, more remarkable results and in less time than if there were originally no indications of that faculty; but even if there were no original indications of individual power, that power can be developed to a high degree through the faithful application of the great law—he can who thinks he can, or to state it differently—one who thinks they can develops the power that can.

There is no faculty that we all do not possess, either in the active or in the latent state. Every faculty that naturally belongs to the human mind is latent in every mind, and it can be awakened and developed, provided the proper laws are faithfully applied. It should be our object, however, to accomplish as much as possible in the present. It is therefore advisable to proceed in the beginning to work through, and develop, those faculties that already indicate considerable power. The mind that has some talent for invention should proceed to think that they can invent. Thus they will accumulate more and more inventive ability or genius. The mind that has some talent for music, should proceed to think that they can master the art of music. They will thereby cause the creative energies of their mentality to accumulate more and more in the faculty of music, until that faculty will be developed to a greater and greater degree. The mind that has some talent for art should apply the same law upon that talent. The mind that has literary ability should proceed to think that they can write what they want to write, and they will finally secure that literary ability or genius with which they can write what they want to write. The mind that has ability in any line of business should proceed to think that they can conduct that business in the most successful manner. Should they enter that business and continue to think that they can, combining such thought with good work, enterprise and the full use of their personal ability, their success will continue to grow indefinitely.

Whatever man may think that he can do, let them proceed to carry out that undertaking, constantly thinking that he can. He will succeed from the beginning, and his advancement will be continuous. However, no mind need be confined to a single purpose. If we have talent for something better than we are doing now, or if we wish to awaken some talent that we long to possess, we may proceed now to think that we can do what we long to do. We shall thus give more and more power to that faculty until it becomes sufficiently strong to be applied in actual practice. In the mean time, we should continue to think that we can do better and better what we are doing now. We shall thereby advance steadily in our present work, and at the same time, prepare ourselves for a greater work in the coming days.

When we think that we can, we must enter into the very soul of that thought and be thoroughly in earnest. It is in this manner that we awaken the finer creative energies of mind, those forces that build talent, ability and genius—those forces that make man great. We must be determined to do what we think we can do. This determination must be invincible, and must be animated with that depth of feeling that arouses all the powers of being into positive and united action. The power that can do what we think we can do will thus be placed at our command, and accordingly we may proceed successfully to do what we thought we could do.

The fact that you have failed to get the lesser proves conclusively that you deserve the greater. So therefore, dry those tears and go in search of the worthier prize.

Count nothing lost; even the day that sees "no worthy action done" may be a day of preparation and accumulation that will add greatly to the achievements of tomorrow. Many a day was made famous because nothing was done the day before.

Know what you want and continue to want it. You will get it if you combine desire with faith. The power of desire when combined with faith becomes invincible.

Some of the principal reasons why so many fail to get what they want is because they do not definitely know what they want or because they change their wants almost every day.

OBSESSION

X
HOW WE SECURE WHAT WE PERSISTENTLY DESIRE

THE purpose of desire is to inform man what he needs at every particular moment to supply the demands of change and growth in his life; and in promoting that purpose, desire gives expression to its two leading functions. The first of these is to give the forces of the human system something definite to do, and the second is to arouse those forces or faculties that have the natural power to do what is to be done.

In exercising its first function, desire not only promotes concentration of action among the forces in man, but also causes those forces to work for the thing that is wanted. Therefore, it is readily understood why the wish, if strong, positive, determined and continuous, will tend to produce the thing wished for. If you can cause all the elements and powers in your being to work for the one thing that you want you are almost certain to get it. In fact, you will get it unless it is so large that it is beyond you, or beyond the power of your present capacity to produce; though in that case you have exercised poor judgment; you have permitted yourself to desire what lies outside of your sphere; and what you could neither appreciate nor use were you to get it.

What you can appreciate, enjoy and use in your present sphere of existence, you have the power, in your present state of development, to produce; that is, you can produce it if all your power is applied in your effort to produce it; and when you desire any particular thing with the full force and capacity of your desire you cause all your power to be applied in producing that particular thing.

In exercising its second function, desire proceeds directly into that faculty or group of forces that can, if fully applied, produce the very thing that is desired. In its first function it tends to bring all the forces of the system together, and inspires them with the desire to work for what is wanted. It acts upon the system in general and gives everything in the system something definite to do, that something definite in each case being the one thing desired. In its second function it acts upon certain parts of the system in particular; always upon those parts that can do what is wanted done; and it tends to arouse all the life and power that those particular parts may contain. How desire proceeds, and how it secures results in this respect is easily illustrated.

We will take, for example, a man who is not earning as much as he feels that he needs. Naturally, he will begin to desire more money; and we will suppose that this desire becomes stronger and stronger until it actually stirs every atom of his being. Now what happens? He is not only arousing a great deal of latent and unused energy, but all of his active energy is becoming more and more alive. But what becomes of all this energy? It goes directly into his moneymaking faculties, and tends to increase decidedly the life, the power, the capacity and the efficiency of those faculties.

There is in every mind a certain group of faculties that is made by nature for financial purposes. In some minds these faculties are small and sluggish, while in other minds they are large and active. And that the latter kind should be able to make more money and accumulate things in a greater measure is quite natural. But is it possible to take those faculties that are small and sluggish and make them large and active? If so, those who now have limited means may in the course of time have abundance.

To answer this question, we will ask what it is that can arouse any faculty to become larger and more active, and we find that it is more energy, and energy that is more alive. No matter how sluggish a faculty may be, if it is thoroughly charged, so to speak, with highly active energy, it simply must become more active. And no matter how small it may be, if it continues to receive a steady stream of added life, energy and power, day after day, month after month, year after year, it simply must increase in size and capacity. And whenever any faculty becomes greater in capacity and more alive in action it will do better work; that is, it will gradually gain in ability and power until it has sufficient ability and power to produce what you wished for.

Returning to the man in our illustration, we will see how the principle works. His money-making faculties are too small and too sluggish to produce as much money as he needs. He begins to desire for more. This desire becomes strong enough to arouse every element and force in his money-making faculties; for here be it remembered that the force of any desire goes directly into that faculty that can, by nature, produce the thing desired. This is one of the laws of mind. In addition, the action of his desire tends to arouse all the other forces of his system, and tends to concentrate those forces upon the idea of making more money.

In the beginning, no important change in his financial ability may be noticed, except that he feels more and more confidence in his power to secure the greater amount desired. In a short time, however, possibly within a few months, he begins to get new ideas about the advancement of his work. His mind is beginning to work more actively upon the idea of increased gain. Accordingly, suggestions as to how he might increase the earning capacity of his business are constantly coming up in his mind, and ways and means and plans are taking shape and form more and more completely.

The actions of his money-making faculties are also beginning to change; that is, they are becoming finer, more penetrating, and more keen so that his insight into financial matters is steadily improving. He is therefore securing the necessary essentials to greater financial gain, and as he applies them all things will naturally begin to take a turn. To state it briefly, his strong, persistent desire for more money has aroused his money-making faculties. They have become stronger, more active, more wide-awake and more efficient. And as a strong, wide-awake faculty can do many times as good work as one that is only partly alive, we understand how his desire for more money has given him the ability to make more money. As he continues this desire, making it stronger and more persistent, his financial ability will increase accordingly, and his financial gains continue to increase in proportion.

Many may doubt the efficiency of the plan just presented, because as is well known, most people desire more money but do not always get it. But do they always wish hard enough? It is not occasional desire, or half-hearted desire that gets the thing desired. It is persistent desire; and persistent desire not only desires continually, but with all the power of life and mind and soul. The force of a half alive desire, when acting upon a certain faculty, cannot cause that faculty to become fully alive. Nor can such a desire marshal all the unused forces of the system and concentrate them all upon the attainment of the one thing wanted And it is true that the desires of most people are neither continuous nor very deep They are shallow, occasional wishes without enough power to stir to action a single atom.

Then we must also remember that results do not necessarily follow the use of a single force. Sometimes the force of persistent desire alone may do wonders but usually it is necessary to apply in combined action all the forces of the human system. The force of desire, however, is one of the greatest of these, and when fully expressed in connection with the best talents we may possess, the thing desired will certainly be secured.

We may take several other illustrations. Suppose you have a strong desire for more and better friends. The action of that desire, if deep, whole-hearted and persistent will tend to impress the qualities of friendship upon every element of your character. In consequence, you will in time become the very incarnation of friendship; that is, you will become a better and a better friend, and he who becomes a better friend will constantly receive more and better friends. In other words, you become like the thing you desire, and when the similarity has become complete you will get what you want through the law of like attracting like.

You may desire to succeed in a certain line of work; we will say, in the literary field. If your desire for success in that field is full and persistent, the power of that desire will constantly increase the life, the activity and the capacity of your literary faculties, and you will naturally do better work in that field. The same is true with regard to any other line of work, because your desire for greater success in your work will arouse to fuller action those faculties that you employ in that work. But, in every case, the desire must be deep, whole-souled, persistent and strong.

It is therefore evident that results in all lines of endeavour depend very largely upon the power of desire, and that no one can afford to let their desires lag for a moment. The law should be: Know what you want, and then want it with all the life and power that is in you. Get your mind and your life fully aroused. Persistent desire will do this. And that it is most important to do this is proven by the fact that in thousands of instances, a partly alive mind is the only reason why the goal in view has not been reached.

It is necessary, however, that your desires continue uninterruptedly along the lines you have chosen. You may desire a score or more of different things, but continue each desire without change, unless you should find that certain changes are necessary to secure the greater results you have in mind. To desire one thing today and another tomorrow means failure. To work for one thing this year and another thing next year is the way to empty handedness at the end of every year.

Before you begin to apply the power of desire, know with a certainty what you want because when you get what you have desired, you may have to take it. If you do not know definitely what you really do want, desire a better judgment, a clearer understanding and a more balanced life. Desire to know what is best for you, and the force of that desire will tend to produce normal action in every part of your system. Then you will feel distinctly what the highest welfare of your nature actually demands.

In deciding upon what you want, however, do not be timid, and do not measure the possible with the yard-stick of general appearances. Let your aspirations be high, only be sure that you are acting within the sphere of your own inherent capacity; though in this connection it is well to remember that your inherent capacity is many times as great as it has been supposed to be; and also that it can be continuously enlarged.

In choosing what you are to desire, act within reason, but go after the best. If the full power of desire is applied upon all the elements of your mind and character, what is latent within you will be aroused, developed and expressed; you will become much more than you are and thereby will not only desire the best, but be able to be of service to the best. And this latter fact is important. When we desire the great and the wonderful we must ask what we have to give the great and the wonderful in return. It is not only necessary to get the best—to realize our ideal, but it is also necessary to be so good and so great that we can give to the best as much as we are receiving from the best. Before we begin to wish for an ideal, we must ask what that ideal is going to get when it comes.

Coupled with our desire for the ideal, therefore, we must have an equally strong desire for the remaking of ourselves so that we may become equal to that ideal in every respect. If we want an ideal companion, we must not only wish for such a companion, but we must also desire the development of those qualities in ourselves that we know would make us agreeable to that companion. If we want a different environment we should wish for such an environment with all the life and soul we possess, and should at the same time wish for the increase of those powers in our own talents that can earn such an environment. If we want a better position we should desire such a position every minute and also desire that we may become more competent to fill it when it comes.

The power of desire not only tends to arouse added life and power in these faculties upon which it may act, but it also tends to make the mind as a whole more alert and wide-awake along those lines. This is well illustrated by the fact that when we have a strong, continuous desire for information on a certain subject, we always find someone or something that can give us that information. And the reason is that all the faculties of the mind are prompted by the force of this desire to be constantly on the look-out for that information .

That the same law will apply in the desire or search for wisdom, new ideas, better plans, better opportunities, more agreeable environments and more ideal companions, is clearly understood. And when we couple this fact with the fact that the power of desire tends to increase the life, the ability, the working capacity and the efficiency of these faculties or forces that can produce what we desire, we must certainly admit that those who have found the secret of using desire have made a great find indeed. But, as stated before, and it cannot be repeated too often, the desire must be persistent and strong, as strong as all the life and soul we possess.

In other words, we must wish hard enough, and we wish hard enough when our desires are sufficiently full and deep and strong to thoroughly arouse those faculties that have the natural ability to fulfil those desires. Many desires are only strong enough to arouse their corresponding faculties to a slight degree—not enough to increase the activity or working capacity of these faculties, while most desires are too weak to arouse any force or faculty in the least.

The act of wishing hard enough, however, does not imply hard mental work. If you make hard work of your wishing, you will use up your energy instead of turning it into those channels where it can be applied to good account. It is depth of desire and fullness of desire combined in an action that is directed continuously upon the one thing desired that constitutes true desire. To wish hard enough is simply to wish for all that you want with all that is in you. But we cannot wish with all that is in us unless our wish is subconscious as well as conscious because the subconscious is a part of us—the larger part of us.

To make every desire subconscious, the subconscious mind should always be included in the process of desire; that is, whenever we express a desire we should think of the subconscious, and combine the thought of that desire with our thought of the subconscious mind. Every desire should be deeply felt as all deeply felt mental actions become subconscious actions.

It is an excellent practice to let every desire sink into the deeper mental life, so to speak; and also to act in and through that deeper mental life, whenever we give expression to desire; or, in other words, when we turn on the full force and power of that desire. To become proficient in these methods requires some practice, though all that is necessary to become proficient is to continue to try. No special rule is required.

Begin by feeling your desires through and through. Make them as strong and as deep as you can, and always combine the living action of your desire with your thought of those faculties through which you know that desire is to work. To illustrate: If you desire greater success in your work, think of those faculties that you are using in your work whenever you give full expression to your desire. If you are a business man, think of your business faculties whenever you desire greater business success. If you are a musician, think of your musical faculties whenever you desire greater proficiency in your music. Though in case your desires should be such that you do not know through what kinds of faculties it will naturally be expressed, never mind. Continue to desire what you want; the power of that desire, if persistent and strong, will find a way to make your wish come true.

When we understand how desire works, and know that it works only when it is persistent, we realize that we have found, not only a great secret, but also a simple explanation for many of the failures in life as well as many of its greatest achievements. And from the facts in the case we conclude that no matter what an individual's condition or position may be today, if they will decide upon that something better that they want, they may get it, provided their wish for it is as strong as their own life and as large as their own soul.

The optimist lives under a clear sky; the pessimist lives in a fog. The pessimist hesitates, and loses both time and opportunity; the optimist makes the best use of everything now, and builds themselves up, steadily and surely, until all adversity is overcome and the object in view realized. The pessimist curbs their energies and concentrates their whole attention upon failure; the optimist gives all their thought and power to the attainment of success, and arouses their faculties and forces to the highest point of efficiency. The pessimist waits for better times, and expects to keep on waiting; the optimist goes to work with the best that is at hand now, and proceeds to create better times. The pessimist pours cold water on the fires of their own ability; the optimist adds fuel to those fires. The pessimist links their mind to everything that is losing ground; the optimist lives, thinks and works with everything that is determined to press on. The pessimist places a damper on everything; the optimist gives life, fire and go to everything. The optimist is a building force; the pessimist is always an obstacle in the way of progress. The pessimist lives in a dark, soggy unproductive world, the optimist lives in that mental sunshine that makes all things grow.

XI

CONCENTRATION AND THE POWER BACK OF SUGGESTION

THE purpose of concentration is to apply all the active forces of mind and personality upon that one thing which is being done now, and it may therefore be called the master key to all attainments and achievement. In its last analysis, the cause of all failure can be traced to the scattering of forces, and the cause of all achievement to the concentration of forces. This does not imply however, that concentration is the only essential, but it does imply that concentration must be perfect, or failure is inevitable no matter how many good methods one may employ. The ruling thought of concentration is, " This one thing I do," and it can be stated as an absolute truth that whenever the mind works completely in the attitude of that thought, concentration is perfect.

The value of concentration is very easily illustrated by taking, for example, a wheel of twenty spokes with every spoke a pipe, and all those pipes connected with another conveying steam. The steam will thereby pass out through twenty channels. Then connect an engine with one of the pipes. That engine will accordingly receive only one-twentieth of the steam conveyed through the wheel, while nineteen-twentieths will pass out in waste. But suppose the other nineteen pipes were plugged so that all the steam would pass out through the one pipe connected with the engine. The engine would then have twenty times as much power as before.

The average mind is quite similar to such a wheel. An enormous amount of energy is generated at the hub, so to speak, or at the vital centre of mental life; but as a rule, that power passes out through a score of channels, so that the channel of action receives only a fraction of the power generated in the human system. But here we must remember that you can apply your power effectively only in one direction at a time; therefore, if all your power is to be applied in that one direction, all other channels must be closed up for the time being; or in other words, all the power of mind and thought must be concentrated where you are acting at the time.

In learning how to concentrate, it is necessary in the beginning to remember that the usual methods are of no value. You cannot develop concentration by fixing thought or attention upon some external object. Real concentration is subjective, and subjective thought is deep; that is, it acts through the deeper or interior realms of mind. When you fix your attention, however, upon some external object, like a spot on the wall, as has been suggested by some would-be instructors in this field, your thought goes out towards the surface, so that you are actually getting away from the true field of concentration. Any method, or any line of thinking that tends to draw the mind out towards the surface, will produce a superficial attitude, and when the mind is in such an attitude, deep mental action is not possible; but deep mental action is absolutely necessary in all concentration. There is no use trying to concentrate unless the action of the mind is deep. That is the first essential. In other words, the mind must go into the psychological field; the mind must act, not on the surface of things, but through the deeper life of its thought process.

To develop concentration, all that is necessary is to apply consciously those two factors that are invariably found in natural concentration. In the conscious application of these two factors, the following two methods will be found sufficient; in fact, nothing further will be required in the attainment of concentration to any degree desired.

The first method is to train the mind to act in the subjective or psychological field; in other words, cause all thinking, all feeling and all actions of thought, will and desire to become deeper and finer; in fact, deepen as far as possible all mental action. Whenever you concentrate or turn your attention upon any subject or object, try to feel deeply, try to think deeply and try to turn thought into deeper realms of feeling. The moment your mental action begins to deepen, you will find your attention directed upon the object in mind with perfect ease and with full force. Whenever you are thinking about anything, try to feel your thought getting into the vital life of that something, and wherever you turn your attention, try to feel that the force of that attention acts through your whole mind instead of simply on the surface of your mind. To state it briefly, whenever you concentrate, deepen your thought, and the deeper your thought becomes, the more perfectly will the full force of your mind and thought focus upon the point of concentration. Whatever you have to do, deepen your thought while giving that work your attention, You will find that you will thereby give all your energy to that work and this is your purpose.

The second method is to become interested in that upon which you desire to concentrate. If you are not interested in that subject or object, begin at once to look for the most interesting point of view. You will be surprised to find that no matter how uninteresting a subject may seem, the very moment you begin to look for the most interesting viewpoints of that subject, you will almost immediately become interested in that subject itself. And it is a well-known fact that whenever we are thoroughly interested in a subject we concentrate thoroughly and naturally upon that subject.

To make concentration perfect, so that you can turn all the power of mind and thought upon any subject or object desired, these two methods should be combined. Always look for the most interesting points of view, and while you are looking for those viewpoints, deepen the action of your mind by trying to feel the real vital life of those actions. You thereby become interested in the subject on the one hand, and you make every action of the mind subjective on the other hand; and when perfect interest is combined with subjective mental action, you have perfect concentration.

The constant practice of these two methods will develop the power of concentration to such an extent that you can concentrate completely at any time and for any length of time, by simply deciding to do so; and that such an attainment is of enormous value is evident when we understand how much power there is in man, and how concentration can turn all of that power upon the one thing that is being done now.

All modern psychologists agree that there is enough power in any man being to accomplish what he has in view, provided it is all constructively applied in that one direction. And when man can concentrate perfectly, he can use all of his power wherever he may choose to act. Then, if he combines scientific thinking and constructive mental action with concentration, nothing can prevent him from realizing his very highest ambition.

Another important essential in the use of the forces of mind and thought, is that of understanding suggestion and the power back of suggestion; and this becomes especially true when we realize that there is no factor or condition that we may come in contact with anywhere or under any circumstances, that does not suggest something.

To define suggestion, it may be stated that anything is a suggestion that brings into mind some thought, idea or feeling that tends to undermine some similar idea, thought or feeling that happens to be in the mind at the time. When you have certain ideas or feelings, and you meet circumstances that tend to remove those ideas or feelings, the power of suggestion is working in your mind. If your mind is in a wholesome state and an unwholesome picture removes that wholesome state by replacing something that is degrading, your mind is in the power of suggestion. If you feel joyous and some idea given to you makes your mind depressed, you are in the hands of suggestion; in fact, when anything enters your mind in such a manner as to remove certain similar or opposite states already in your mind, it exercises the power of suggestion.

It is therefore necessary to understand how this power works, so that we can take advantage of good suggestions and avoid those that are not good. The great majority are receiving all sorts of suggestions every hour, and they respond to a very large number of them; in fact, we can truthfully say that most people are controlled, most of the time, by suggestions that come to them from their environment. Those minds, however, who understand the power of thought, and who know the difference between detrimental and beneficial suggestions, can close their minds to the former and open them fully to the latter. And the method to apply is this, that whenever you are in the presence of an adverse suggestion, concentrate your attention upon some idea or mental state which you know will act as a counter suggestion; in other words, when adverse suggestion is trying to produce in your mind what you do not want, persist in suggesting to yourself what you do want. This practice, if employed frequently, will soon make you so strong in this direction that you will unconsciously, so to speak, be on your guard; in fact, the very moment that an adverse suggestion is given, your mind will spring up of its own accord with a wholesome suggestion to meet the requirements. To avoid becoming a victim to adverse suggestions—and we have such suggestions about us almost constantly—fill your mind so full of good, wholesome thoughts and suggestions that there is no room for anything else. Feel right at all times, and nothing from without can tempt you to think wrong. Make every good thought subconscious, and no adverse thought from without can possibly get into your subconscious mind at any time.

A great many suggestions do not produce results, a fact which should be perfectly understood, because every thought that we think does contain some suggestion. When we are trying to impress good thoughts upon our minds, we want the good suggestions conveyed by those thoughts to take effect, but frequently they do not, and the reason is that a suggestion takes effect only when we exercise the power that is back of suggestion. The outward suggestion itself is simply the vehicle through which another power is acting, and that other power is nothing more nor less than the real life of that idea which the suggestion intends to convey.

To simplify this matter, we will suppose that you are suggesting to yourself that you are well. The suggestion itself is simply a vehicle conveying the idea of health, but if your mind is not in touch with the interior or living force of that idea of health at the time you are giving the suggestion, you have not exercised the power back of suggestion, and the idea of health will not be conveyed to your subconscious mind. On the other hand, if you can actually feel the power of this interior idea of health when you are giving the suggestion, you are in mental touch with the power back of that suggestion, and whenever you touch the power back of suggestion you use that power. Results, therefore, will be forthcoming. To explain further, we might say that you use the power back of suggestion whenever you mentally feel that vital idea which the suggestion aims to convey. When you feel that idea, you respond to the suggestion, but when you do not feel it, you do not respond.

This explains why the power of suggestion so frequently fails, not only in everyday life, but also in mental healing. When you think health, you will produce health in your system if you feel the real or interior life of health at the time. When you think harmony you will produce harmony in your system, if your mind actually goes into the soul of harmony at the time. When you place yourself in the mental world of happiness whenever you are thinking happiness, you will actually produce happiness in your mind, because you are applying the power that is back of the thought that suggests happiness.

Two men may present the same proposition under the same circumstances, and you will accept the proposition from the one, while ignoring the arguments of the other completely. The reason will be that while the one is talking about his proposition, the other is talking through his proposition. The mind of the one goes on the outside of his arguments and his suggestions, while the mind of the other goes through the real inner life of those arguments and suggestions. Therefore, the one is only using suggestion, while the other is also using the power back of suggestion; and it is the power back of suggestion that produces results, whenever results are secured. The same idea is illustrated when a person is speaking on a certain subject. If his description deals simply with the shell of that subject, he does not attract attention, but the moment he touches the vital or inner factors of that subject, everybody is interested. The reason is, he has touched the power back of his theme. But we all have ideas or suggestions to present at frequent intervals. Therefore, if we can use the power back of our suggestion at such times we may receive a hearing, but if we cannot, we attract little or no attention.

Thus we understand the value of knowing how to use the power back of suggestion, and we can learn to use this power by training ourselves to get into the real life of every idea and every thought that we may try to think or convey. When we try to live our ideas and thoughts, we will begin to express that interior power, and we shall succeed in living our ideas when we try to feel consciously and constantly the real life and the real truth that is contained in those ideas.

To secure the best results from the power of thought in its various modes of application, we must understand that there is something back of everything that takes form or action in life, and that it is through this something that the actions of mind should move whenever we use thought or suggestion in any manner whatever. When we are conscious only of the body of our ideas, those ideas convey no power. It is when we become conscious of the soul of those ideas that we have aroused that something within that alone produces results in the mental world. Any thought or suggestion that conveys simply the external form, invariably falls flat. There is nothing to it. It is entirely empty, and produces no impression whatever. But our ideas and suggestions become alive with the fullness of life and power when we also convey the real life or the real soul that is contained within the body of those thoughts. We have, at such times, entered the depths of mental life. We are beginning to act through undercurrents, and we are beginning to draw upon the immensity of that power that exists in the vast interior realms of our own mental world.

Say to yourself a hundred times every day, and mean it with all your heart: I will become more than I am. I will achieve more and more every day because I know that I can. I will recognize only that which is good in myself, only that which is good in others; only that in all things and places that I know should live and grow. When adversity threatens I will be more determined than ever in my life to prove that I can turn all things to good account. And when those whom I have trusted seem to fail me, I will have a thousand times more faith in the honour and nobleness of man. I will think only of that which has virtue and worth. I will wish only for that which can give freedom and truth. 1 will expect only that which can add to the welfare of the race. I will live to live more. I will speak to give encouragement, inspiration and joy. I will work to be of service to an ever-increasing number. And in every thought, word and action my ruling desire shall be, to enrich, ennoble and beautify existence for all who come my way.

XII
THE DEVELOPMENT OF THE WILL

N O force in the human system can be properly used unless it is properly directed, and as the will is the only factor in man that has the power to direct or control, a thorough development of the will, as well as a clear understanding of its application under every circumstance, becomes absolutely necessary if we are to use all the forces within us to the very best advantage.

To define the will with absolute exactness is hardly possible, though a clear knowledge as to its general nature and special functions must be secured. In a previous chapter, it was stated that the "I Am" is the ruling principle in man, and it may be added here that when the "I Am" exercises this function of rulership anywhere in the human system, will power is the result; or, it may be stated that the will is that attribute of the "I Am" which is employed whenever there is a definite intention followed by actual action, with a view of initiating, controlling or directing. To state it briefly therefore, will power is the result of the "I Am" either taking initiative action or controlling and directing any action after it has been taken.

Among the many functions of the will, the principal ones are as follows: The will to initiate; the will to direct; the will to control ; the will to think; the will to imagine; the will to desire; the will to act; the will to originate ideas; the will to give expression to those ideas; the will to will into action any purpose, the will to carry through that purpose; the will to employ the highest and most perfect action of any force or faculty in mind; and the will to push up, so to speak, any talent in the mind to its highest point of efficiency. This last mentioned function has been ignored, but it is by far the most important in the practical life of attainment and achievement.

To illustrate this idea, we will suppose that you have a group of faculties, all of which are well developed, and contain a great deal of ability and power. But how can those faculties be caused to act? The fact is they will not act in the least until the will wills them into action. The will therefore must first be applied, but the act of initiating action among those faculties is not its only function. To illustrate again, we will suppose that your will is very weak. It therefore stands to reason that the original impulse given those faculties will also be weak. Then when we understand that it is necessary for the will to continue to prompt or impel the continued action of any faculty we realize how weak, half-hearted and limited such an action will necessarily be when the will is weak. On the other hand, if your will is very strong, the original impulse given to the faculty will be strong and the continued action of that faculty will be much stronger, larger and more efficient. In brief, when a faculty is backed up, so to speak, with a powerful will, it easily doubles its capacity and efficiency; in other words, it is pushed up to a higher state of action. We understand therefore the great importance of having a strong will, though such a will is not only an advantage in promoting a fuller and larger expression of any faculty we may possess, but also in promoting a larger and more perfect expression of any force that may be applied, either in the personality, in character or in mind.

A powerful will, however, is never domineering or forceful. In fact, a domineering will is weak. It may be seemingly strong on the spur of the moment, but it cannot be applied steadily for any length of time. A strong will, however, is deep, continuous, and persistent. It calls into action your entire individuality, and as you exercise such a will you feel as if a tremendous power from within yourself had been calmly, though persistently aroused.

When we analyse the human mind, in the majority we find the will to be weak, and in fact, almost absent in a great many. Such people do not have the power to take a single original step. They have no initiative, and accordingly drift with the stream. Among others, who are a little higher in the mental scale, we find a will somewhat stronger, but not sufficiently strong to exercise with any degree of efficiency a single one of its functions. Among what can be called "the better class," we invariably find the will to be fairly well developed, and among the great leaders in all the different phases of human life and action, we find the will to be very strong in fact, there is not a single mental or spiritual giant in history, who did not have a tremendous will, and this was one their great secrets.

To illustrate further with regard to the last mentioned of the special functions, we will suppose that you have some talent for music. If you should will to exercise that talent to a slight degree only, it is evident that your efficiency along that line would not be marked. On the other hand, if your will was so strong that you could push up, so to speak, your musical faculty to its very highest point of efficiency, you would soon find yourself on the verge of musical genius; in fact, musical genius is absolutely impossible unless you have a strong will, no matter how much musical talent you may possess. Though it must be remembered in this connection that it is not sufficient simply to have a strong will.

The majority do not possess a strong will, and most of those who do have a strong will, have not learned how to apply it so as to secure greater efficiency in anything they may do; and here it is important to state that anyone who will increase the power of their will, and properly train it for the purpose just indicated, may expect to increase their efficiency anywhere from twenty-five to two hundred per cent. The majority have many times as much ability and working capacity as they are using at the present time; in fact, they apply only a small fraction of what is in them, and the principal reason why they do not apply all that is in them, is that they do not have sufficient power of will to act on this larger scale.

In this connection, we find another condition which is very important, and especially with regard to overcoming circumstances. A great many people have good intentions, and they have sufficient will power to originate those intentions, but they have not sufficient will power to carry them out; in other words, they have the will to think, but not the will to act. And here we can use our own imagination in picturing that state of human affairs that would inevitably come into being if all good intentions became actions.

Thousands of people start out right, but they have not the power of will to continue, so that where ten thousand make a good beginning, less than a score finish the race. We find this condition in all walks of life and in all undertakings, and it illustrates most eloquently the necessity of a strong will in every mind.

Realizing the importance of a strong will, and knowing that the will is weak in the minds of the great majority, we may well ask what might be the cause of this weakness; and the answer is that there are several marked causes, all of which we shall proceed to consider.

The first among these causes is alcohol. The use of alcohol weakens the will, not only in the individual who partakes of it, but in their children and grandchildren, and many generations following. It has been estimated by those who have studied this subject carefully, that the use of alcohol from generation to generation through the centuries is one of the principal causes for this weakness in the human will that we find to be almost universal. And when we study the psychology of the subject we soon discover the reason why.

Nearly every nation, as far back in history as we can go, has been using alcohol in some form or other, and as its weakening effect upon the will is transmissible from one generation to another, we realize that practically every member of the race has been burdened, more or less, with this adverse inheritance. But in this connection, we must remember that it is not necessary to be disturbed by this dark picture, because no matter what we have inherited, we can overcome it absolutely. However, we do not wish to do anything that will be in our own way, or in the way of generations that are to follow. It is therefore necessary that we consider this subject thoroughly, and act upon it accordingly.

The fact that the human race has transmitted a weak will from generation to generation explains why the human family does not have enough power to produce more than an occasional mental giant. Here and there we find in history, men and women who tower above the rest. Their minds are strong, their wills powerful, and their souls invincible; but how different is the condition among the majority. Most of them constitute mere driftwood, and follow blindly the leadership of these mental giants the race has produced. This, however, is not the intention of nature. Nature intends all men and women to be mental and spiritual giants, and does not intend that any one should follow the will of another. But the human race has, in this respect, ignored the intentions of nature.

The reason why the use of alcohol weakens the will, is very easily explained. When you take anything into the system that tends to take control over your desires, feelings or intentions, you permit yourself to be controlled by an outside agency, and accordingly the will for the time being is laid aside; and the law is, that whenever the will is laid aside by anything whatever it is weakened; that is, you undermine, so to speak, that element of the will which gives it the power to direct and control. When this practice is continued and repeated a number of times, we can readily understand how the power of the will is gradually decreased more and more, until its very foundation has been practically removed.

When you permit an outside agency to control your feelings and emotions at frequent intervals for a prolonged period, your system will soon get into the habit of submitting to the control of this outside agency, and will not respond any longer to any effort that the will may make to regain its original power of control. This being true, we find an explanation for a number of perplexing questions. We learn why great men and women are not more numerous. We learn why the majority are so easily influenced by temptations. We learn why powerful characters are found only here and there, and we also learn why every great nation of past history has fallen.

When we study history, we find that every great nation, after coming to a certain point of supremacy, began to decline, and there are several reasons for this strange termination of national power. But there is only one reason that stands out as the most vital of them all, and as possibly the cause of them all. We refer to the fact that a decrease of great men and women invariably precedes the decline of a nation. To keep any great nation up to a high standard of civilization there must be enough superior characters to hold the balance of power, but the very moment the balance of power gets into the hands of second grade men and women, a decline of that nation is inevitable. Therefore, if any great nation in the present age is to continue to grow in real greatness and real power, we must make a special effort to increase the number of great men and women in every generation. The greater a nation becomes, the more great men and women are required to govern and direct the forces of progress and growth that are at work in that nation. We therefore understand what is required of us in this generation if we want present civilization to advance and rise in the scale.

Another cause of this weakness in the will is found in what may be called psychical excess. And it is unfortunate that so many people have permitted themselves to be placed under psychical influences during the last fifty or seventy-five years; though it is a fact that a great many people have permitted their minds to be controlled or influenced by the psychical or the occult in every age. Another tendency therefore towards weakness in the will has been transmitted from generation to generation down through the ages, and we all have the effect of this misuse of mind also to overcome at the present time; but again let us remember that we have the power to overcome anything that we might have inherited.

Whenever you give up your individuality, or any part of your mind or thought, to some unknown force or influence that you know little or nothing about you are permitting an outside agency to usurp the function of the will. You lay the will aside, you undermine its power to some extent, and thereby weaken those elements in its nature that constitute self-mastery and self-control. That psychical excess has this tendency to a most pronounced degree is well illustrated by the fact that every individual, who is fascinated with psychical experience, invariably lacks in self-control. Such people are usually so sensitive that they are swayed in every direction by every suggestion or influence or environment with which they may come in contact.

But here we may well ask what we are living for—if we are living to give up to the influence of environment, visible or invisible, or if we are living to attain such full control over the powers and talents that are within us, that we can not only control, modify, and perfect environment, but also so perfectly control ourselves that we can become all that nature intends that we should become. If we are to rise in the scale, we must attain greater degrees of self-mastery, but we cannot learn to master ourselves so long as we are constantly permitting ourselves to be mastered by something else; and those who indulge in psychical experiences to any degree whatever, are permitting themselves to be mastered by something else. They are therefore losing ground every day. Their characters are becoming weaker, their standards of morality and rightness becoming more and more lax, as we all have discovered, and their power to apply those faculties and forces in their natures through which they may accomplish more and achieve more, are constantly decreasing both in working capacity and in efficiency.

If man wants to live his own life as it should be lived; if he wants to master circumstances and determine his own destiny, he must have the power to say under all sorts of conditions what he is going to think and what he is going to do; but he cannot exercise this power unless his own will is permitted to have absolute control over every thought, effort and desire in his life.

Emotional excess is another cause that weakens the will, and by emotional excess we mean the act of giving way to uncontrolled feelings of any kind. To give way to anger, hatred, passion, excitability, intensity, sensitiveness, grief, discouragement, despair, or any other uncontrolled feeling, is to weaken the will. The reason is that you cannot control yourself through your will when you permit yourself to be controlled by your feelings; and any act that rules out the will, weakens the will.

Whenever you permit yourself to become angry, you weaken the will. Whenever you permit yourself to become offended or hurt you weaken your will. When-

:ver you permit yourself to become despondent or discouraged, you weaken your vill. Whenever you give way to grief, mental intensity or excitability, you weaken /our will. You permit some artificial mental state to take possession of your mind, ind your will at the time is put aside. We therefore should avoid absolutely all :motional excess. We must not permit any feeling whatever to take possession of is, or permit ourselves to be influenced in any form or manner by anything that nay enter the mind uncontrolled through the emotions; but this does not mean hat we should ignore emotion. Emotion is one of the most valuable factors in iuman life, and should be used and enjoyed under every normal circumstance,)ut should never become a ruling factor in mind, thought or feeling.

You may look at a beautiful picture, and lose yourself, so to speak, in its charms. You may listen to exceptional music, and be carried away, or be thrilled through ind through by the joy of its harmony; or you may witness some scene in nature .hat causes your soul to take wings and soar to empyrean heights. You may per-nit yourself to enjoy any or all of these ecstasies at anytime, provided you have :onscious control over every movement of your emotions at the time.

Whenever you feel the touch of some sublime emotion, try to direct the force)f that emotion into a finer and a higher state of expression; thus you will not)e controlled by it, but will exercise control over it, and accordingly will enjoy :he pleasure of that emotion many times as much. It is a well-known fact that vhenever we control any feeling, whether it be physical or mental or spiritual, and :ry to turn it into a larger sphere of expression, we enjoy far more the pleasure :hat naturally comes through the exercise of that feeling. To control our emotions :herefore is to lose nothing and gain much.

Another cause of weakness in the will is what might be called mental depend-:nce. To depend upon anybody or anything outside of yourself, is to weaken :he will, for the simple reason that you let the will of someone else rule your ictions, while your own will remains dormant. Nothing, however, that remains lormant can grow or develop. On the other hand, it will continue to become veaker and weaker, like an unused muscle, until it has no strength whatever. We :herefore understand why those multitudes of people, who have followed blindly :he will and leadership of others, not only in religion but in all other things, have practically no will power at all. And here we wish to state that it is positively wrong for any individual or any group of individuals to follow any one man or any one woman or any group of men or women under any circumstances whatever. We are here in this life to become something. We are here to make the best use of what we possess in mind, character and personality, but we cannot cause any element, faculty or power within us to express itself to any extent so long as we are mere dependent weaklings.

In everything, depend upon yourself, but work in harmony with all things. Do not depend even upon the Infinite, but learn to work and live in harmony with the Infinite. The highest teachings of the Christ reveal most clearly the principle that no soul was created to be a mere helpless instrument in the hands of Supreme Power, but that every soul should act and live in perfect oneness with that Power. And the promise is that we all are not only to do the things that Christ did, but even greater things. Man is no credit to Supreme Creative Power if he remains in the puppet stage, but he is a credit to that Power if he becomes a giant in character, mind and soul. In our religious worship we have given unbounded praise to God for His wonderful power in creating man, and the very next moment we have announced the hymn, "Oh To Be Nothing." The absurdity of it all is too evident

73

to need comment, but when we understand that character and manhood, as well as practical efficiency in life, are the products of strength and not of weakness, we must come to the conclusion that every system of thought in the present age, be it religious, moral, ethical, or philosophical, needs complete reconstruction.

We are here to become great men and women, and with that purpose in view, we must eliminate everything in our religion and philosophy that tends to make the human mind a dependent weakling. If you would serve God and be truly religious, do not kneel before God, but learn to walk with God, and do something tangible every day to increase the happiness of mankind. This is religion that is worthwhile, and it is such religion alone that can please the Infinite.

Another cause which is too large and diversified to outline in detail, is that of intemperance; that is immoderation in anything in life. To indulge excessively any desire or appetite, be it physical or mental, is to weaken the will. Partake only of that which is necessary and good, and observe moderation. Control yourself under all circumstances, and resolve never to go too far in anything, because too much of the good may be more of an evil than not enough of it.

The effects of weakness in the will are numerous, but there are two in particular that should receive marked attention. The first is that when the will is weak, the human system becomes incapable of resisting temptations, and therefore moral weakness or a complete moral downfall is inevitable. Character in the largest sense of the term is impossible without a strong will, and it is impossible to accomplish anything that is of permanent value without character.

The second is that weakness in the will inevitably implies weak mental actions; that is, no matter how much ability you may possess, if your will is weak, you will apply only a fraction of that ability; and there are thousands of able men and women who are failures in life simply because they have not the will to apply all their ability. If they would simply increase the power of their will, and properly train that will, they would immediately pass from failure to success, and in many instances, remarkable success. It is the power of the strong will alone that can give full expression to every talent or faculty you may possess, and it is only such a power that can push up the actions of every faculty to a point of high efficiency.

In learning to develop the will and to use the will, realize what the will is for. Understand clearly what its functions actually are, and then use it in all of those functions. Avoid anything and everything that tends to weaken the will, and practice every method known that can strengthen the will. Do not give in to any feeling or desire until you succeed in directing that feeling or desire as you like. Feel only the way you want to feel, and then feel with all the feeling that is in you. Whatever comes up in your system, take hold of it with your will and direct it so as to produce even greater results than were at first indicated. Use the will consciously as frequently as possible in pushing up your faculties to the highest point of efficiency; that is, when you are applying those faculties that you employ in your work, try to will them into stronger and larger actions. This is a most valuable practice, and if applied every day will, in the course of a reasonable time, not only increase the capacity and ability of those faculties, but will also increase decidedly the power of the will.

Whenever you will to do anything, will it with all there is in you. If no other practice than this were taken, the power of the will would be doubled in a month. Depend upon the power that is in you for everything, and determine to secure the results you desire through the larger expression of that power. Never give in to anything that you do not want. When a certain desire comes up that you do not care to entertain, turn your attention at once upon some favourable desire, and give all the power of your will to that new desire. This is very important, as the average person wastes more than half of their energy entertaining desires that are of no value, and that they do not intend to carry out. When ever any feeling comes up in the system ask yourself if you want it. If you do not, turn your attention in another direction; but if you do want it, take hold of it with your will and direct it towards the highest states of mind that you can form at the time. In brief, every action that enters the system, whether it comes through thought, feeling, desire or imagination, should be redirected, by the power of the will and turned into higher and greater actions.

Whenever you think, make it a practice to think with your whole mind. Make your thinking whole-hearted instead of halfhearted. Whenever you act, act with all there is in you. Make every action firm, strong, positive and determined; in other words, put your whole soul into everything that you feel, think or do. In this way, you turn on, so to speak, the full current of the will, and whenever the will is used to its full capacity, it will grow and develop.

Try to deepen every action of mind and thought; that is, do not think simply on the surface, but also think subconsciously. Think and act with your deeper mental life. You thereby give the power of the will a deeper field of action, and it is established in the larger life of your individuality instead of in the surface thought of your objective mind. The difference between a superficial will and a deeply established will is readily found in everyday experience. When you will to do anything and your intentions are easily thwarted by the suggestion of someone else, your will is on the surface. But when your intentions are so deeply rooted in the subconsciousness of your mind that nothing can thwart those intentions, your will has gained that great depth which you desire.

The more easily you are disturbed, the weaker your will, while the stronger the will, the more difficult it is for anything to disturb your mind. When the will is strong, you live and exercise self-control in a deeper or interior mental world, and you look out upon the confusions of the outer world without being affected in the least by what takes place in the external.

Whenever you exercise the will, try to place the action of that will as deeply in the world of your interior mental feeling as you possibly can; that is, do not originate will-action on the surface, but in the depth of your own supreme individuality. Try to feel that it is the "I Am" that is exercising the power of the will, and then remember that the "I Am" lives constantly upon the supreme heights of absolute self-mastery. With this inspiring thought constantly in mind, you will carry the throne of the will, so to speak, farther and farther back into the interior realms of your greater mental world, higher and higher up into the ruling power of the supreme principle in mind. The result will be that you will steadily increase the power of your will, and appropriate more and more the conscious control of that principle in your greater nature through which all the forces in your possession may be governed and directed.

He who would become great must live a great life.

Happiness adds life, power, and worth to all your talents and powers. It is most important, therefore, that every moment should be full of joy.

However much you may do, always remember you have the ability to do more. No one has as yet applied all the ability in their possession. But all of us should learn to apply a greater measure every year.

While you are waiting for an opportunity to improve your time, improve yourself.

The man who never weakens when things are against him, will grow stronger and stronger until he will have the power to cause all things to be for him.

THE WING

XIII
THE BUILDING OF A GREAT MIND

A GREAT mind does not come from ancestors, but from the life, the thought and the actions of the individual; and such a mind can be constructed by anyone who understands the art of mind building, and who faithfully applies this art.

You may have a small mind today, and your ancestors for many generations back may have been insignificant in mental power; nevertheless, you may become even exceptional in mental capacity and brilliancy if you proceed to build your mind according to the principles of exact science; and those principles anyone can apply.

There are two obstacles, however, that must be removed before this building process can begin, and the first one of these is the current belief in heredity. That we inherit things is true, but the belief that we cannot become any larger or any better than our inheritance is not true. As long as a person believes that greatness is not possible to them because there were no great minds among their ancestors, they are holding themselves down, and cannot become any more than they subconsciously think they can; while on the other hand, the person who expects to become much because they had remarkable grandfathers is liable to be disappointed because they depend too much upon their illustrious forefathers and not enough upon themselves. Blood will tell when combined with ambition, energy and enterprise, but the very best of blood will prove worthless in the life of one who expects ancestral greatness to carry them through. When we have received good things we must turn them to good account or nothing is gained. Our success will not come from the acts of our forefathers, but can come alone from what we are doing now.

Those who have inherited rich blood can use that richness in building greatness in themselves, but those who have not the privilege of such inheritance need not be discouraged. They can create their own rich blood and make it as rich as they like. Whether your forefathers were great or small matters not. Do not think of that subject, but live in the conviction that you may be come what you wish to become by using well the good you have received, and by creating those essentials that you did not receive. If you have inherited undesirable traits, remember that evil is but valuable power misdirected. Learn to properly direct all your forces and your undesirable traits will be transformed into elements of growth, progress and advancement.

We all have met men and women with remarkable talents who persisted in thinking that they would never amount to anything because there was no genius among their ancestors. But if there had been a genius in the family some time during past generations, the question would be where that genius actually received their genius. If we all have to get greatness from ancestors, where did the first great ancestor get their greatness? There must be a beginning somewhere to every individual attainment, and that beginning might just as well be made by us now. What others could originate in their time, we can originate in our time.

The belief that we must inherit greatness from someone in order to attain greatness is without any scientific foundation whatever, and yet there are thousands of most promising minds that remain small simply because they entertain this belief.

To believe that heredity is against you and that you therefore will not accom-

77

plish anything worthwhile, is to make your work a wearing process instead of a building process. In consequence, you will not advance, and you will constantly remain in the rear; but the moment you realize that it is in your power to become as much as you may desire, your work and study will begin to promote your own growth and advancement. When you live, think and act in the belief that you can become much, whatever you do will cause you to become more. Thus all your actions will develop power and ability, and living itself will become a building process.

That man may become great regardless of the fact that there were no great minds among his ancestors many thinkers will admit, provided there are indications of exceptional ability in the man himself, but they entertain no hope if they see nothing in the man himself. And here we have the second obstacle to the building of a great mind. This obstacle, however must be removed in every mind that aims to rise above the ordinary, because the belief that the average person has nothing in them is the cause of fully three-fourths of the mental inferiority we find in the world. But the new psychology has conclusively demonstrated the fact that the man or woman who has nothing in them does not exist. All minds have the same possibilities, though most of those possibilities may be dormant in the minds of the majority.

The difference between a great mind and a small mind is simply this, that in the former the greater possibilities have come forth into objective action, while in the latter those possibilities are still in subjective inaction. When we say that a man has nothing in them we are contradicting the very principle of existence, because to be a man, a man must have just as much in him as any other man. What is in him may not be in action, and his mentality may appear to be small, but the possibilities of greatness are there. There is a genius somewhere in his mind, because there is a genius in every mind, though in most minds that genius may as yet be asleep.

When every child is taught the great truth that it has unlimited possibilities within its own subconscious mind, and that it can, through the scientific development of those possibilities, become practically what it may desire to become, we shall have laid the foundation for the greatest race of people that the ages have known. But we need not wait for future generations to demonstrate the possibilities of this truth. Every mind that begins to apply the principle of this truth now may begin to enlarge their mind now, and they may continue this process of enlargement indefinitely.

When we have removed the two obstacles mentioned and have established ourselves in the conviction that we have unlimited possibilities within us, more than sufficient to become whatever we may desire, we are ready to proceed with the building of a great mind.

To promote the building of a great mind, the two prime essentials, scope and brilliancy, must be constantly kept in the foreground of consciousness. The mind that is not brilliant is of little value even though its scope may be very large. Likewise, the mind that is narrow or circumscribed is extremely limited, however brilliant it may be. A great mind is great both in capacity and ability. It can see practically everything and see through practically everything. To see everything is to have remarkable scope. To see through everything is to have exceptional brilliancy.

To give scope to the mind, every action of mind must be trained to move toward that which is greater than all persons or things. Those feelings or desires that cause the mind to become absorbed in some one thing or group of things, will limit the mental scope. Therefore in love, sympathy, and purpose the sphere of action must be universal. When we live only with that love that centres attention upon a limited number of persons, one of the greatest actions of mind will work in a limited world. When our sympathies go only to a chosen few, the same thing occurs, and when our purpose in life has a personified goal, we keep the mind within the limitations of that personification.

To give universality to our feelings and actions, may require considerable training of the mental tendencies, but it is absolutely necessary if we will develop a great mind. It is only those mental forces that move towards the verge of the limitless in every direction that can cause the mind to transcend limitations; therefore, all the forces of the mind should be given this transcending tendency.

To develop mental scope, consciousness must move in every direction, and it must move along right lines, so that no obstacle may be met during that continuous expansive process. Such obstacles, however, are always produced by limitations of thought. Therefore, they may be avoided when all the actions of mind are placed upon a universal scale. In the mental actions of love, we find many forces, all of which are true in their own places, but all of these forces must be exercised universally; that is, they must act upon a scale that is without bounds in the field of your own consciousness. The mind must go in every direction as far as it possibly can go in that direction, and must act in the conviction that wherever it may go it can go farther still. The understanding must know that there is no obstacle where the mind may seem to cease in its onward action, and that the mind is forever growing, thereby going as far each day as that day's development requires.

When this idea is applied to a personal love between man and woman, the feeling of love must be based upon the principle that those two souls have the power to love each other more and more indefinitely; that the larger the love becomes the more lovable will the objects of that love become, and that the consciousness of perfect unity in pure affection increases constantly as the two souls become more and more individualized in their own sublime nature. It is possible to make conjugal love universal and continuous between one man and one woman when the love of each is directed toward the sublime nature of the other. Through this law, each individual develops through the consciousness of the largeness of the real nature of the other, and the more the two love each other in this universal sense, the more they will see in each other to love. In addition, the minds of both will constantly enlarge in scope, because when love acts upon this larger scale, the whole mind will act upon this larger scale, as there is no stronger power in mind than love.

The love between parent and child can, in like manner, be made universal. In this attitude, the parent will love all of the child, not only the visible person, but the undreamed-of wonders that are waiting in that child-mind for expression. The child already loves the parent in this larger sense, and this is one reason why the child-mind lives so much nearer to the limitless, the universal, the ideal and the beautiful. And when the parent will do likewise, there will arise between the two a love that sees more and more to love the more love loves in this larger, sublime sense.

The idea is not only to love the tangible, but also that other something that transcends the tangible—that something that appears to the soul in visions, and predicts wonders yet to be. That such a love will expand and enlarge the mind anyone can understand, because practically all the elements of the mind will tend to follow the actions of the love nature, when that nature is exceptionally strong. But we must not imagine that we shall, through this method, love the person less. The fact is, we shall love the person infinitely more, because we shall discern more and more clearly that the person is the visible side of that something in human life that we can only describe as the soul beautiful—that something that alone can satisfy the secret longings of the heart.

The love of everything can, through the same law, become universal. Even friendship, which is always supposed to be confined to a small world, may become universal and limitless in the same way; and when it does, you will see more to admire in your friend every day. You will both have entered the boundless in your admiration for each other, and having entered the boundless, you will daily manifest new things from the boundless, and thus become delightfully surprised at each other constantly. The same may be employed in making sympathy universal; that is, never sympathise with the lesser, but always sympathise with the greater. The lesser is combined in the greater, and by sympathising with the greater, the mind becomes greater.

In the fields of motives, objects, aims and purposes, we find that nearly every mental action is occupying a limited scope, and is acting in such a manner that its own limitations are being perpetuated. This tendency, however, must be removed if a greater mind is to be constructed, because every action of the mind must aim to change itself into a larger action. To cause every aim or purpose to become universal in its action, the mind must transcend shape, form, space and distance in its consciousness of everything that it may undertake to do. When we confine our thought to so far or so much, we place the mind in a state of limitations, but when we promote every object with a desire to go as far as the largest conception of the present may require, and proceed to attain as much as present capacity can possibly appropriate, we are turning all purposes and aims out upon the boundless sea of attainment. And we shall not only accomplish all that is possible in our present state of development, but we will at the same time constantly enlarge the scope of the mind.

It is absolutely necessary to have a fixed goal whatever our purpose in life may be, but we must never give special shape or size to that goal. We must think of our goal as being too large to be measured, even in the imagination. When we have a goal in mind that is only so and so large, all the creative energies of the mind will limit themselves accordingly. They will create only so and so much, regardless of the fact that they may be able to create many times as much. But when we think of our goal as being too large to be measured, the creative energies will expand to full capacity, and will proceed to work for the largest attainment possible. They will act constantly on the verge of the limitless, and will cause the mind to outdo itself every day.

In the field of desire, the same law should be applied, and applied constantly, as there are no actions in the mind that exercise a greater influence over the destiny of man than that of desire. When desire is low or perverted, everything goes down or goes wrong, but when desire changes for the better, practically everything else in the human system changes to correspond. To train desire to become universal in action, every individual desire should be changed so as to set only for the promotion of growth. Those desires which when fulfilled, do not make for the enlargement of life, are detrimental. The power of all such desires therefore must be changed in their course. Your object is to become more and achieve more, and to constantly promote that object, development and growth must be perpetual throughout your system. For this reason, every action must have growth, for its purpose, and as every action is the result of some desire, no desire must be permitted that is not conducive to growth. It is not necessary, however, to remove a single desire from the human system to bring about this change, because every desire can be trained to promote the building of a greater life.

When every desire is caused to move towards the larger and the greater through the mind's irresistible desire for the larger and the greater, all the creative forces of the mind will move towards the same goal, and will constantly build a greater mind. The principle is this, that when all the actions of mind are trained to move towards the larger, they will perpetually enlarge. The first essential to the building of a great mind will thereby be promoted.

To promote the second essential, mental brilliancy, the actions of mind must be made as high and as fine as possible; that is, the vibrations of the mental life must be in the highest scale attainable. To see through everything the mind will require the very finest rays of mental light, and as this mental light is produced by the vibrations of the actions of mind, these actions should be as high in the scale as we can possibly reach at every stage of our mental ability. The light of intelligence is created by the mind itself, and the more brilliant this light becomes, the greater will become the powers of intelligence, discernment, insight, understanding, ability, talent and genius. And the power of mind to create a more brilliant mind increases as the mind places itself more and more in the consciousness of the absolute light of universal intelligence.

To cause the mind to become more brilliant, all the tendencies of mind should fix their attention upon the highest mental conception of mental brilliancy. Every expression of the mind should be animated with a refining tendency. Every force of the mind should rise towards the absoluteness of mental light. Those states of mind that tend to magnify the inferior must be eliminated, and this is accomplished by thinking only of the superior that is possible in all things. All mental actions that are critical, depressing or depreciative must be replaced by their constructive opposites, as every action of the mind must concentrate its attention upon the largest and the best in all fields of consciousness. The mind must be kept high in every respect, because the higher in the mental scale the mind functions, the more brilliant will become the mental light.

To increase the rapidity of the vibrations in these higher mental states, creative energy must be supplied in abundance, and to comply with this requirement, all that is necessary is to retain in the human system all the energy that is already created. The human system creates and generates an enormous amount of creative energy every day. Therefore, when all this energy is retained and transmuted into finer mental elements, the mind will be abundantly supplied with those finer energies that can increase both the power and the brilliancy of thought and mind. The mind that is animated with a strong desire to constantly refine itself, and that is thoroughly charged with creative energy, will always be brilliant, and will become more and more brilliant as the laws given above are faithfully and thoroughly applied.

Remove the sting; remove the whine; remove the sigh. They are your enemies. They are never conducive to happiness; and we all live to gain happiness, to give happiness. From every word remove the sting. Speak kindly. To speak kindly and gently to everybody is the mark of a great soul. And it is your privilege to be a great soul. From the tone of your voice remove the whine. Speak with joy. Never complain. The more you complain, the smaller you become, and the fewer will be your friends and opportunities. Speak tenderly, speak sweetly, speak with love. From all the outpourings of your heart, remove the sigh. Be happy and contented always. Let your spirit sing, let your heart dance, let your soul declare the glory of existence, for truly life is beautiful. Every sigh is a burden, a self-inflicted burden. Every whine is a maker of trouble, a forerunner of failure. Every sting is a destroyer of happiness, a dispenser of bitterness. To live in the world of sighs is to be blind to everything that is rich and beautiful. The more we sigh, the less we live, for every sigh leads to weakness, defeat, and death. Remove the sting, remove the whine, remove the sigh. They are not your friends. There is better company waiting for you.

XIV
HOW CHARACTER DETERMINES CONSTRUCTIVE ACTION

ALL the elements of life are good in themselves; and should produce good results when in action; that is, when the action is properly directed; but when any action is misdirected, evil follows, and this is the only cause of the ills of human existence.

Everything that is wrong in the world has been produced by the perversion and the misuse of the good. Therefore, to eliminate wrong, man must learn to make the proper use of those things that exist in his sphere of action. The misuse of things comes either from ignorance or lack of character, or both. That person who does not understand the elements and the forces of the world in which they live will make many mistakes, and will make the wrong use of nearly everything unless they are guided by instructions of those who understand. The leadership of greater minds is therefore necessary to the welfare of the race, but this leadership is not sufficient. Guidance from great minds will help to a limited degree so long as the actions of the individual are simple, but when greater development is sought, with its more complex actions, the individual must learn to master the laws of life for themselves. They can no longer depend upon others.

Therefore, though the leadership of greater minds be necessary to the welfare of the race, it is also necessary for that leadership to be used, not for keeping the multitude in a state of simple-mindedness and dependence, but for promoting the intelligence of each individual until external guidance is needed no more. The true purpose of the strong is to promote greater strength in the weak, and not to keep the weak in that state where they are at the mercy of the strong. Our united purpose should be to develop more great men and women, and to do everything possible to lead the many from dependence to independence.

Every state of individual attainment is preceded by a childhood period, but this period should not be unnecessarily prolonged, nor will it be, when every strong mind seeks to develop strength in the weak instead of using the weakness of the weak for their own gain. Those who understand the laws of life may inform the ignorant what to do and what not to do, and may thereby prevent most of the mistakes that the ignorant would otherwise make. But this guidance will not prevent all the mistakes, as experiences demonstrate, because it requires a certain amount of understanding to even properly apply the advice of another. Those who do not have the understanding will therefore misuse the elements of life at every turn, no matter how well they are guided by wiser persons, while those who do have this understanding will invariably begin to do things without consulting their so-called superiors. It is therefore evident that more understanding for everybody is the remedy, as far as this side of the subject is concerned, but there is also another side.

A great many people go wrong because they do not know any better. To them, a better understanding of life is the path to emancipation. They will be made free when they know the truth, but the majority of those who go wrong do know better. Then why do they go wrong? The cause is lack of character. When you fail to do what you want to do, your character is weak. The same is true when you preach one thing and practice another. When you fail to be as perfect, as good or as ideal as you wish to be, or fail to accomplish what you think that you can accomplish, your character is at fault. It is the character that directs the action of the mind. It is the lack of character, or a weak character that produces misdirections; and when you fail to accomplish what you feel you can accomplish, something is being misdirected.

What you feel that you can do that you have the power to do. Therefore, when you fail to do it, some of the powers of your being are being misdirected. To be influenced to do what you would not do if you were normal, means that your character is weak, and to be affected by surroundings, events, circumstances and conditions against your will indicates the same deficiency. A strong character is never influenced against their will. They are never disturbed by anything, never become upset, offended or depressed. No one can insult them because they are above small states of mind, and stronger than those things that may tend to produce small states of mind. All mental tendencies that are antagonistic, critical or resisting indicate a deficiency in character. The desire to criticise becomes less and less as the character is developed. It is the mark of a fine character never to be critical and to mention but rarely the faults of others. A strong character does not resist evil, but uses their strength in building the good. They know that when the light is made strong, the darkness will disappear of itself. A strong character has no fear, never worries and never becomes discouraged. If you are in the hands of worry, your character needs development. The same is true if you have a tendency to submit to fate, give in to adversity, give up in the midst of difficulties, or surrender to failure or wrong. It may be stated, without any exceptions or modifications whatever, that the more temper, the less character. Anger is always misdirection of energy, but it is the function of character to properly direct all energies. Therefore, there can be no anger when the character is thoroughly developed.

The mind that changes easily, that is readily carried away by every new attraction that may appear, and that does not retain a well-balanced attitude on any subject lacks character. A strong character changes gradually, orderly, and only as each step is thoroughly analysed and found to be a real step forward. The more individuality, the more character, and the more one is oneself, the stronger the character. Practice being yourself, your very best self, and your very largest self, and your character will be developed. The more one is conscious of flaws and defects, the weaker the character, and the reason is because nearly everything is being misdirected when the character is weak. The strong character is conscious only of the right because such a character is right, and is causing everything in its sphere of action to do right.

To the average person, character is not important as far as this life is concerned; and as most theological systems have declared that it was repentance and not character that would insure human welfare in the world to come, the development of character has naturally been neglected. But when we realize that it is character that determines whether our actions in daily life are to go right or wrong and that every mistake is due to a lack of character, we shall feel that the subject requires attention.

It is the power of character that directs everything that is done in the human system or by the human system. Character is the channel through which all expressions must pass. It is character that gives human life its tone, its colour and its quality, and it is character that determines whether our talents and faculties are to be their best or not.

The man who has a well-developed character is not simply good. He is good for something, because he has the power to turn all his energies to good account. A strong character not only turns all the elements and energies of life to good account, but has the power to hold the mind in the right attitude during the most trying moments of life, so that they will not make mistakes nor fall a victim to insidious temptation. A strong character will keep all the faculties and forces of life moving in the right direction, no matter what obstacles we may meet in the way. We shall turn neither to the right nor to the left, but will continue to move directly towards the goal we have in view, and will reach that goal without fail.

Thousands of people resolve every year to press on to higher attainments and greater achievements. They begin very well, but before long they are turned off the track. They are misled or switched off by counter attractions. They have not the character to keep right on until they have accomplished what they originally set out to do. True, it is sometimes wisdom to change one's plans, but it is only lack of character to change one's plans without reason, simply because there is a change of circumstance. To change with every circumstance is to drift with the stream of circumstance and those who drift can only live the life of a log. He will be victim of every external change that he may meet. He will control little or nothing, and he will accomplish little or nothing.

We all can develop the power to control circumstances or rather to cause all circumstances to work with us and for us in the promotion of the purpose we have in view; and this power is character. Never permit circumstances to change your plans, but give so much character to your plans that they will change circumstances. Give so much character to the current of your work that all things will be drawn into that current, and that which at first was but a tiny rivulet, will thus be swelled into a mighty, majestic stream.

When the various forces of the system are properly directed and properly employed, the development of the entire mentality will be promoted; and this means greatness. The power that directs the forces of the system is character, and it is character that causes the mind to use those forces in the best and most instructive manner. There must be character before there can be true greatness, because any deficiency in chraracter causes energy to be wasted and misdirected. It is therefore evident that the almost universal neglect in the development of character is one of the chief reasons why great men and women are not as numerous as we should wish them to be. Many may argue, however, that great minds do not always have good characters, and also that some of our best characters fail to manifest exceptional ability. But we must remember that there is a vast difference between that phase of character that simply tries to follow the moral law, and real character—the character that actually is justice, virtue and truth. Then we must also remember that character does not mean simply obedience to a certain group of laws, but the power to use properly all the laws of life. That person who uses mental laws properly, but fails to comply with moral laws does not possess a complete character. Nevertheless, the character of this person is just as good as that of the person who follows moral laws while constantly violating mental laws.

In the study of character, it is very important to know that the violation of mental laws is just as detrimental as the violation of moral laws, though we have been in the habit of condemning the latter and excusing the former. That person who uses properly the mental laws, will to a degree promote the development of the mind even though they may neglect the moral laws; and this accounts for the fact that a number of minds have attained a fair degree of greatness in spite of their moral weakness. But it is a fact of extreme importance, that those minds who attain greatness in spite of their moral weakness could become two or three times as great if they had also developed moral strength. That person who complies with the mental laws but who violates the moral laws, wastes fully one-half of the energies of their mind, and sometimes more. His attainment and achievement will, therefore, be less than one-half of what they might be if he had moral character as well as mental character.

The same is true, however, of that person who complies with the moral laws, but who violates the mental laws; fully one-half of their energy is wasted and misdirected. This explains why the so-called good characters are not any more brilliant than the rest, for though they may be morally good, they are not always mentally good; that is, they do not use their minds according to the laws of mind, and therefore cannot rise above the level of the ordinary.

The true character tries to turn all the energies of the system into the best and most constructive channels, and it is the mark of a real character when all the various parts of the being of man are working together harmoniously for the building of greatness in mind and soul. When the character is weak, there is more or less conflict among the mental actions. Certain actions have a tendency to work for one thing, while other actions are tending to produce the very opposite. The same is true of the desires. A character that lacks development will desire one thing today, and something else tomorrow. Plans will change constantly, and little or nothing will be accomplished. In the strong character, however, all actions work in harmony and all actions are constructive. And this is natural because it is the one supreme function of character to make all actions in the human system constructive—to make every force in the human life a building force.

Be good and kind to everybody and the world will be kind to you. There may be occasional exceptions to this rule, but when they come pass them by and they will not come again.

Ideals need the best of care. Weeds can grow without attention, but not so with the roses.

Not all minds are pure that think they are. Many of them are simply dwarfed.

It does not pay to lose faith in anybody. It is better to have faith in everybody and be deceived occasionally than to mistrust everybody and be deceived almost constantly.

When you meet a person who does not look well, call their attention to the sunny side of things, and aim to say something that will give them new interest and new life. You will thereby nip in the bud many a threatening evil, and carry healing with you wherever you go.

XV
THE ART OF BUILDING CHARACTER

CHARACTER is developed by training all the forces and elements of life to act constructively in those spheres for which they were created, and to express themselves in those actions only that promote the original purpose of the being of man.

Every part of the human system has a purpose of its own—a purpose that it was created to fulfil. When those elements that belong to each part express themselves in such a way that the purpose of that part is constantly promoted, all actions are right; and it is character that causes those actions to be right. Character is therefore indispensable, no matter what one's object in life may be. Character is the proper direction of all things, and the proper use of all things in the human system. And the proper use of anything is that use that promotes the purpose for which that particular thing was created.

To develop character it is therefore necessary to know what life is for, to know what actions promote the purpose of that life, and to know what actions retard that purpose. When the secret of right action is discovered, and every part of man is steadily trained in the expression of right action, character may be developed. But whatever is done, character must be applied in its fullest capacity. It is only through this full use, right use and constant use that anything may be perpetuated or developed.

Character develops through a constant effort to cause every action in the human system to be a right action; that is, a construetive action, or an action that promotes the purpose of that part of the system in which the action takes place. This is natural because since character is the power of right action, every effort to extend the scope of right action will increase the power of character. To have character is to have the power to promote what you know to be the purpose of life, and to be able to do the right when you know the right. To have character is to know the right, and to be so well established in the doing of the right that nothing in the world can turn you into the wrong.

The first essential is therefore to know the right; to be able to select the right; to have that understanding that can instinctively choose the proper course of action, and that knows how each force and element of life is to be directed so that the original purpose of human life will be fulfilled. The understanding of the laws of life will give this first essential in an intellectual sense, and this is necessary in the beginning; but when character develops, one inwardly knows what is right without stopping to reason about it. The development of character enables one to feel what is right and what course to pursue regardless of exterior conditions or intellectual evidence. The intellect discerns that the right is that which promotes growth and development; character inwardly feels that the right leads to greater things and to better things, and that the wrong leads invariably to the inferior and the lesser.

The presence of character produces a consciousness of growth throughout the system; and the stronger the character, the more keenly one can feel that everything is being reconstructed, refined, perfected and developed into something superior, This is but natural because when the character is strong, everything in the system is expressed in right action, and the right action of anything causes the steady development of that particular thing.

To distinguish between the right and the wrong becomes simplicity itself when one knows that the right promotes growth, while the wrong retards growth. Continuous advancement is the purpose of life; therefore, to live the right life is to live that life that promotes progress and growth, development and advancement in everything that pertains to life. For this reason, that action that promotes growth is in harmony with life itself, and must consequently be right. But that action that retards growth is at variance with life; therefore it is wrong; and wrong for that reason alone. Everything that promotes human advancement is right. Everything that interferes with human advancement is wrong. Here we have the basis of a system of ethics that is thoroughly complete, and so simple to live that nobody need err in the least.

An intellectual understanding of the laws of life will enable anyone to know what action promotes growth and what action retards growth, but as character develops, one can feel the difference between right and wrong action in one's own system, because the consciousness of right becomes so keen that anything that is not right is discerned at once. It is therefore evident that the power to distinguish the right from the wrong in every instance will come only through the development of character. No matter how brilliant one may be intellectually, he cannot truly know the right until he has a strong character. The external understanding of the right can be misled, but the consciousness of the right is never mistaken; and this consciousness develops only as character develops.

The second essential is to create a subconscious desire for the right—a desire so deep and so strong that nothing can tempt the mind to enter into the wrong. When this desire is developed, one feels a natural preference for the right; to prefer the right, under all circumstances becomes second nature, while every desire for the wrong will disappear completely. When every atom in one's being begins to desire the right, the entire system will establish itself in the right attitude, and right action will become the normal action in every force, function and faculty. In addition, this same desire will produce mental tendencies that contain the power of right action, which always means constructive action.

It is a well known fact that all the forces and energies of the system, and all the movements of mind follow mental tendencies; therefore, when the mental tendencies are right actions, everything that takes place in the system will produce right action; and everything will be properly directed.

The desire for the right may be developed by constantly thinking about the right with deep feeling. Every thought that has depth, therefore, will impress itself upon the subconscious, and when that thought is inspired with a strong desire for the right, the conscious impression will convey the right to the subconscious. Every impression that enters the subconscious will cause the subconscious to bring forth a harvest of that which the impression conveyed; therefore, when the right is constantly held in mind with deep feeling, the right thought will soon become the strongest in the mind; and our desires are the results of our strongest thoughts.

You always desire that which is indicated in your strongest thought. You can therefore change those desires completely by thinking with deep feeling about that which you want to desire. No desire should be destroyed. All desires should be transmuted into the desire for the right, and when you subconsciously desire the right, every action in your being will be a right action.

The two fundamental essentials, therefore, to the development of character are to know the right and to desire the right, but the term "right" as employed here must not be confounded with that conception of right which includes only a few of the moral laws. To be right according to the viewpoint of completeness, is to be in harmony with all the principles of life, and all the laws of the present sphere of human existence. To know the right, it is necessary not simply to memorize rules that other minds have formulated, but to inwardly discern what life is for, and what mode of thought and action is conducive to the realisation of that which is in life. To desire the right, according to this view of the right, the mind must actually feel the very soul of right action, and must be in such perfect touch with the universal movement of right action, that all lesser and imperfect desires are completely swallowed up in the one desire—the desire that desires all that is in life, and all that is in perfect harmony with that which is in life.

It is the truth, that when we come into perfect touch with the greater, we cease to desire the lesser, and the closer we get to the one real desire, the less we care for our mistaken desires. Therefore, to remove an undesirable desire, the course is not to resist that desire, but to cultivate a greater and a better desire, along the same line. In this connection, we must remember that the adoption of a greater desire does not compel us to sacrifice those things that we gain from the lesser desires. He who adopts the greater loses nothing, but is on the way to the gaining of everything.

To know the right and to desire the right, according to the complete significance of the right we must interiorly discern the very right itself. We cannot depend upon another's definition of the right, but must know fully the spirit of the right with our own faculties. That faculty that knows and feels the right, and that naturally knows and desires the right is character. Therefore, it is through the development of character that each individual will know for themselves how to live, think and act in perfect harmony with the laws of all life.

When the consciousness of right action has been attained, a clear mental picture should be deeply impressed upon mind and every desire should be focused upon that picture. This concentration should be made as strong as possible, so that all the energies of the system are not only aroused, but caused to move towards the ideal of right action. And by right action, we mean that action that is thoroughly constructive, that builds for greater things and greater things only. Everything is right that builds for greater things. If it were not right, it could not produce the greater.

To clearly picture upon the mind the image of right action, and to concentrate with strong desire the whole attention upon that mental image, will cause all the tendencies of mind to move in the same direction. There will therefore be perfect harmony of mental action, and that action will be right action, because everything that moves towards the right must be right. This mental picture of right action should always be complete; that is, one's mental conception of the right should not be confined to certain parts of the system only, but should include every action conceivable in the being of man.

That person who pictures themselves as virtuous, but forgets to picture themselves above anger, fear and worry, is not forming a complete picture or ideal of the right. They are not giving the creative energies of the system a perfect pattern; the character that those energies are to build will therefore be one-sided and weak.

First ask yourself what you would have all the energies, powers, functions and faculties in your system do. Answer that question in the best manner possible, and upon that answer, base your picture of right action. Whenever a new line of action is undertaken, the mind should continue in that original line of action until the object in view has been reached. To do this in all things, even in trivial matters, will not only cause every action to produce the intended results, but real character will steadily be made stronger thereby.

The habit of giving up when the present task is half finished and try something else is one of the chief causes of failure. The development of a strong character, however, will remove this habit completely. To constantly think of the highest and the greatest results that could possibly follow the promotion of any undertaking or line of action will aid remarkably in causing the mind to keep on. To expect much from what we are doing now is to create a strong desire to press on towards the goal in view. To press on towards the goal in view is to reach the goal, and to reach the goal is to get what we expected.

An essential of great importance in the building of character is the proper conception of the ideal. No mind can rise higher than its ideals, but every mind can realize its ideals no matter how high they may be. Our ideals therefore cannot be too high. The ideal should not only be a little better than the present real, but should be perfection itself. Have nothing but absolute perfection in all things as the standard and the goal, and never think of your goal as anything less. Do not simply aim to improve yourself in just one more degree. Aim to reach absolute perfection in all your attainments and all your achievements, and make that desire so strong that every atom in your being thrills with its power.

To form all one's ideals in accordance with one's mental conception of absolute perfection, will cause the mind to live above the world of the ordinary, and this is extremely important in the building of character. A great character cannot be developed so long as the mind continues to dwell on the ordinary, the trivial or the superficial. Neither can true quality and true worth find expression so long as thought continues on the common plane; and the life that does not continue to grow into higher quality and greater worth has not begun to live. When character is highly developed, both the personality and the mentality will feel the stamp of quality and worth. High mental colour will be given to every characteristic, and the nature of man will cease to be simply human. It will actually be more.

In building character, special attention must be given to hereditary tendencies or those traits of character that are born in us. But as all such traits are subconscious, they can be changed or removed by directing the subconscious to produce the opposite characteristics or tendencies. It matters not in the least what we may have inherited from our ancestors. If we want to change those things, we can do so. The subconscious will not only respond to any direction that we may make, but is fully capable of doing anything in the world of mind or character that we may desire to have done. Examine the tendencies of your mind and character, and fix clearly in consciousness which ones you wish to remove and which ones you wish to retain. Those that you wish to retain should be made strong by daily directing the subconscious to give those tendencies more life, more power and more stability. To remove those tendencies that you do not wish to retain, forget them. Do not resist them nor try to force them out of the mind. Simply forget them and direct the subconscious to create and establish new tendencies that are directly opposite to the nature of the ones that you wish to remove. Build up those qualities that constitute real character, and every bad trait that you have inherited from your ancestors will disappear.

To build up those qualities, picture in your mind the highest conceptions of those qualities that you can possibly form; then impress those conceptions and ideas upon tile subconscious. Such impressions should be formed daily and

90

especially before going to sleep as the building process in the subconscious is more perfect during sleep.

By impressing the idea of spotless virtue upon the subconscious every day for a few months, your moral tendencies will become so strong that nothing can tempt you to do what you know to be wrong. Not that physical desire will disappear; we do not want any natural desire to disappear, but your control of those desires will be so complete that you can follow them or refuse to follow them just as you choose. And your desire to remain absolutely free from all wrong will become so strong that nothing can induce you to do what your finer nature does not wish to have done.

There are millions of people who are morally weak in spite of the fact that they do not wish to be, but if these people would employ this simple method, their weakness would soon disappear, because by impressing the idea of spotless virtue upon the subconscious, the subconscious will produce and express in the personality the power of virtue; and if this process is continued for some time, the power of virtue in the person will become so strong that it can overcome and annihilate instantly every temptation that may appear.

Impress upon the subconscious the idea of absolute justice, and your consciousness of justice will steadily develop until you can discriminate perfectly between the right and the wrong in every imaginable transaction. Whatever quality you wish to develop in your character, you can increase its worth and its power steadily by applying this subconscious law; that is, what is impressed upon the sub conscious will be expressed through the personality, and since the seed can bring forth ten, thirty, sixty and a hundred fold, one tiny impression, therefore, may have the power to bring forth a great and powerful expression. Everything multiplies in the subconscious, whether it be good or otherwise. Therefore, by taking advantage of this law and giving to the subconscious only those ideas and desires that have quality and worth, we place ourselves in the path of perpetual increase of everything good that the heart may desire.

The two predominating factors in character are justice and virtue. The former gives each element in life its proper place. The latter turns each element to proper use. The consciousness of justice is developed through the realisation of the fact that nothing can use what is not its own. To try to use what is not one's own will result in misuse.

When the consciousness of justice is thoroughly developed, everything in the human system will be properly placed. That very power of the mind that feels justice—the true placing of things—will cause all things within man to be properly placed. And when justice rules among all things in the interior life of man, that man will naturally be just to all things in the exterior life.

It is not possible for any person to deal justly with people and matters in the external world until he has attained the consciousness of justice within himself. He may think he is just, or may try to be just, but his dealings will not be absolutely just until he can feel justice in his own life. To feel justice within oneself is to keep the entire system in a state of equilibrium. The mentality will be balanced and no force or element will be misplaced. It is therefore something for which we may work with great profit.

To be virtuous in the complete sense of the term, is to use all things properly, and the proper use of things is that use that works for greater things. Virtue is therefore applicable to every force, function and faculty in the being of man, but in its application there must be no desire or effort to suppress or destroy. Virtue

91

means use—right use—never suppression.

When things cannot be used in their usual channels, the energies in action within those things should be turned in their courses and used elsewhere. When creative energy cannot be properly applied physically, it should be employed metaphysically; and all energy can be drawn into mind for the purpose of building up states, faculties, talents or powers. (Practical methods through which this may be accomplished will be given in the next chapter.)

When a certain desire cannot be expressed with good results in its present purpose, the power of that desire should be changed and caused to desire something else—something of value that can be carried out now. The power of that desire therefore is not lost, neither is enjoyment sacrificed, because all constructive forces, give joy to the mind. "And the greatest of joys shall be the joy of going on."

The desire for complete virtue is developed through the realization of the fact that the greatest good comes only when each part fulfils, physically and metaphysically, what nature intended. In the application of virtue, the purpose of nature may be fulfilled metaphysically when the physical channel does not permit of true expression at the time; though when physical expression may be secured, the metaphysical action should always be in evidence, because the greatest results always follow when physical and metaphysical actions are perfectly combined.

In the building of character, the two principal objects in view should be the strong and the beautiful. The character that is strong but not beautiful may have force, but cannot use that force in the building of the superior. The character that is beautiful but not strong will not have sufficient power to carry out its lofty ideals. It is the strong and the beautiful combined that builds mind and character, and that brings into being the superior man.

When the creative energies are daily transmuted, and turned into muscle, brain and mind, a virtuous life can be lived without inconvenience. Besides, the body will be healthier, the personality stronger and the mind more brilliant.

Hold yourself constantly in a positive, masterful attitude, and fill that attitude with kindness. The result will be that remarkable something that people call personal magnetism.

Creative energy when retained in the system will give vigour to the body, sparkle to the eye, and genius to the brain.

There is enough power in any man to enable him to realize all his desires and reach the highest good he has in view. It is only necessary that all of this power be constructively applied.

XVI
THE CREATIVE FORCES IN MAN

THE human system may well be termed a living dynamo, as the amount of energy, especially creative energy, generated in the mind and personality of man is simply enormous. If we should try to measure the amount produced in the average healthy person, we should become overwhelmed with surprise; though we should naturally become even more surprised after learning how much power nature gives to man, and then finding that he applies only a fraction of it. We shall soon see the reason for this, however, and learn exactly why all of this vast amount of energy is not turned to practical use.

What is called creative energy in its broadest, largest sense, is that power in man that creates, forms or reproduces anywhere in the human system, and it divides itself into a number of groups, each one having its special function. One group creates thought, another brain cells, another nerve tissues, another muscular tissues, another manufactures the various juices of the system, another produces ideas, another creates talent and ability, another reproduces the species, and a number of other groups produce the various chemical formations in the system. We therefore have all kinds of creative processes going on in the human system, and corresponding energies with which these processes are continued.

One of the most interesting facts in connection with this study is that Nature generates more energy for each group than is required for normal functioning through its particular channel. In consequence, we find a great deal of surplus energy throughout the system. Each function supplies a certain percentage, and as it is not used by the function itself, the larger part of it naturally goes to waste. And here is where our subject becomes decidedly important. All kinds of creative energy are so closely related that they can be transformed and transmuted into each other. What is wasted in one function can therefore be turned to actual use in another function. An extra supply can thereby be secured for the creation of thoughts and ideas if such should be necessary, or an extra supply can be secured for the manufacture of the different juices of the system, or for the increase of muscular activity or functional activity in any one of the vital organs. Each group will readily change and combine with any other group, thus producing additional power in any part of the system at any time.

More than half of the energy generated in the human system is surplus energy, and is not needed for normal functioning, either in mind or body, though there are many personalities that generate so much energy that fully three-fourths of the amount generated is surplus. The question is therefore what shall be done with this surplus energy, and how any amount of it can be applied through any special function or faculty desired? If a person can accomplish a great deal, sometimes remarkable things by only using a fraction of his energy, it is evident that he could accomplish a great deal more if some means could be found through which he might apply all of his energy. In fact, if such means were found, his working capacity, as well as his ability, might be doubled or trebled, and his achievements increased in proportion. If a certain amount of energy produces a certain degree of working capacity, twice as much energy would naturally double that working capacity, and this has been demonstrated a number of times. A great many people, who have tried to transmute their creative energies, and direct those energies into some special faculty, have found that the working capacity of that faculty has been increased for the time being to a remarkable degree, but this is not the only result secured. The same process will also increase the brilliancy of the mind, and here let us remember that genius, in most instances, is accounted for by the fact that practically all of the surplus energy of the personality flows naturally into that faculty where genius is in evidence.

To illustrate the idea further, take two men of equal personal power. Let one of them permit his surplus energy to flow into the different functions as usual, giving over a part to normal requirements, and the other to mere waste. We shall not fmd this man doing anything extraordinary. But let the other man give over to normal functions only what is actually required, and then turn the remainder into his mind, or those parts of his mind that are being applied in his work. We shall find in this second case that ability will rapidly increase, and that in the course of time actual genius be developed. That genius could be developed by this process in every case, has not been demonstrated, though it is quite probable that it could be demonstrated with out a single exception. However, no individual can turn surplus energy into any faculty without becoming more able, more efficient and more competent in that faculty. To learn how this process can be carried out successfully under any circumstances is therefore thoroughly worthwhile.

To proceed, we must first learn how these different groups of creative energy naturally act; and we find that each group goes, either naturally or through some habit, into its own part of mind or body; in other words, we find in the human system, a number of streams of energy flowing in different directions, performing certain functions on their way, using up a fraction of their power in that manner, the rest flowing off into waste. Knowing this, the problem before us is to learn how to redirect those streams of energy so as to turn them to practical use where they can be used now, and thus not only prevent waste, but increase the result of our efforts in proportion. In brief, we want to know how we can take up all surplus energy, that is, all energy that remains after normal functioning has been provided for, and use that surplus in promoting more successfully the work in which we are engaged. And to learn how to do this, we must study the art of transmutation.

What we call transmutation is not some mysterious something that only a few have the power to understand and apply, but one of the simplest things in Nature, as well as one of the most constant of her processes. Nature is continually transmuting her energies, and it is in this manner that extraordinary results are found anywhere in the realms of Nature, or anywhere in human nature where unconscious actions along greater lines have been the cause. Whenever any individual has accomplished more than usual, it is the law of transmutation through which the unusual has been secured. The use of the law may have been unconscious, though everything that is applied in past and unconsciously, can be applied fully and thoroughly through conscious action.

When anyone is using his mind continually along a certain line, and is so thoroughly absorbed in that line of action that it takes up his whole attention, we invariably find that the mind while in that condition, draws an extra amount of energy from the body. Sometimes it draws too much, so that every desire of the body is, for the time being, suspended and the vitality of the different physical organs decreased below normal. A man while in this condition frequently loses desire for food, and we all know of inventors who have been so absorbed in their experiments that they have neither taken nor desired food for days. We have also found the same condition in many others, especially among authors, composers and artists, where the mind was given over completely to the subject at hand. And what is the cause but transmutation? When the mind takes up for its own use a great deal of the energy naturally employed in the body, the power of normal functioning will have so decreased that the desire for normal functioning will have practically disappeared for the time being.

Another illustration with which we are all familiar, is where every natural desire of the body disappears completely, for a time, when the mind is completely absorbed in some entirely different desire; and here we frnd the law that underlies the cure of all habits. If you would turn your mind upon some desire that was directly opposite to the desire that feeds your habit, and if you would give over your whole attention to that opposite desire, you would soon draw all the energy away from that desire which perpetuates the habit. The habit in question therefore would soon die of starvation. In the same way, people who are inclined to be materialistic could overcome that tendency entirely by concentrating attention constantly and thoroughly upon the idealistic side of life. In this case, those forces of the system that are perpetuating materialistic conditions would be transmuted into finer energies, and would thereby proceed to build up idealistic or more refined conditions of body, mind and personality. Both Nature and human experience are full of illustrations of transmutation, so that we are not dealing in this study with something that lies outside of usual human activity. We are dealing with something that is taking place in our systems every minute, and we want to learn how to take better control of this something, so that we can apply the underlying law to the best advantage.

In learning to apply the law of transmutation, our first purpose should be to employ all surplus energy either in promoting our work or in developing faculties and talents. This process alone would practically double the working capacity of any mind, and would steadily increase ability and talent; and also to turn energy to good account that cannot be used in its own channel now.

To illustrate, suppose you have a desire for a certain physical or mental action, and you know that it would not be possible to carry out that desire at the time. Instead of permitting the energy that is active in that desire to go to waste, you would turn that energy into some other channel where it could be used to advantage now. Our second purpose should be to direct all surplus energy into the brain and the mind in case we had more energy in our body than we could use, or that was required for physical functioning, and thereby become stronger and more efficient in all mental activities. Our third purpose should be to transmute all reproductive energy into talent and genius when there was no need of that energy in its own particular sphere. And in this connection, it is well to mention the fact that a man who is morally clean, other things being equal, has in every instance, greater agility, greater capacity, and greater endurance by far than the man who is not. While the latter is wasting his creative energies in useless pleasures, as well as in disease producing habits, the former is turning all of his creative energy into ability and genius, and the result is evident. In carrying out these three purposes we can prevent all waste of mental and personal power. We can control our desires completely; we can eliminate impurity, and we can turn life and power into channels that will invariably result in greater mental power and brilliancy, if not marked ability and rare genius.

To experiment, turn your whole attention upon your mind for a few minutes, and desire gently to draw all your surplus energy into the field of mental action. Then permit yourself to think along those lines where the mind is inclined to be most active. In a few moments you will discover the coming of new ideas and in many instances, you will for several hours receive ideas that are brighter and more valuable than what you have received for some time. Repeat the process later, and again and again for many days in succession, and it will be strange indeed, if you do not finally secure a group of ideas that will be worth a great deal in your special line of thought or work. Whenever you feel a great deal of energy in your system, and try to direct it into the mind, you will have the same result. Ideas will come quick and rapidly, and among them all you will surely find a few that have exceptional merit.

In learning the art of transmutation, the first essential is to train your mind to think that all surplus energy is being turned into the channel you have decided upon; that is, if you are a business man, you naturally will want all your surplus energy to accumulate in your business faculties. To secure this result, think constantly of your surplus energy as flowing into those faculties. This mode of thinking will soon give your energies the habit of doing what you desire to have done. It is a well-known law, that if we continue to think deeply and persistently along a certain line, Nature will gradually take up that thought and carry it out. Another law of importance in this connection is that if we concentrate attention upon a certain faculty or upon a certain part of the system, we create a tendency among our energies to flow towards that faculty or part. We understand therefore the value of constantly hearing in mind the idea that we wish to realize. What we constantly impress upon the mind through our thoughts and desires, finally becomes a subconscious habit, and when any line of action becomes a subconscious habit, it acts automatically; that is it works of itself.

Before taking up this practice, however, it is necessary to determine positively what you actually desire your surplus energy to do. You must know what you want. Then continue to want what you want with all the power of desire that you can arouse. Most minds fail in this respect. They do not know with a certainty what they wish to accomplish or perfect. Their energies therefore are drawn into one channel today and another tomorrow, and nothing is finished. If you are an inventor, train your mind to think that all your surplus energy is constantly flowing into your faculties of invention. If you are a writer, train your mind to think that all your surplus energy is flowing into your literary talents; or whatever it is that you may be doing or want to do, direct your energy accordingly. You will soon find that you will increase in power, ability, and capacity along the lines of your choice, and if you continue this process all through life, your ability will continue to increase, no matter how long you may live.

The second essential is to desire deeply and persistently that all your surplus energy shall flow into those functions or faculties that you have selected for greater work. Wherever your desire is directed, there the force of your system will also tend to go, and herein we find another reason why persistent desire has such extreme value. The use of desire in this connection, however, must always be deep and calm, and never excited or overwrought.

The third essential is to place your mind in what may be termed the psychological field, and while acting in that field, to concentrate upon that part or faculty where you want your surplus energy to accumulate. This essential or process constitutes the real art of transmutation, though it is by no means the easiest to acquire. To master this method a great deal of practice will be required, but whenever you can place your mind in the psychological field and concentrate subjectively upon any part of your system where you want surplus energy to accumulate, all your surplus energy positively will accumulate in that part within a few moments' time. Through the same process, you can annihilate any desire instantaneously, and change all the energy of that desire into some other force. You can also, in the same way, reach your latent or dormant energies, and draw all of those energies into any channel where high order of activity is desired; in fact, through this method, you can practically take full possession of all the power, active or latent, in your system, and use it in any way that you may wish. That you should, after you learn to apply this method successfully, become highly efficient in your work, is therefore evident, though this is not all. Extraordinary capacity, mental brilliancy and genius can positively be developed through the constant use of this method, provided, however, that nothing is done, either in thought, life or conduct, to interfere with the underlying law of the process.

To place your mind in the psychological field, try to turn your conscious actions into what may be termed the finer depths of the personality; that is, try to become conscious of your deeper life; try to feel the undercurrents of mind and thought and consciousness, and try to act in perfect mental contact with those deep, underlying forces of personality and mentality that lie at the foundation of your conscious activity. An illustration in this connection will be found valuable. When you listen to music that seems to touch your soul, so that you can feel the vibrations of its harmony thrill every atom of your being, you are in the psychological field. You are alive in another and a finer mental world, a mental world that permeates your entire personal existence. You are also in the psychological field when you are stirred by some emotion to the vefy depth of your innermost life. A deepening of thought, feeling, life and desire will take the mind, more or less, into the psychological field; and whenever the mind begins to act in that field, you should concentrate your attention upon that faculty or part of your system where you wish extra energy to accumulate. Make your concentration alive, so to speak, with interest, and make every action of that concentration as deep as possible, and all your surplus energy will positively flow towards the point of concentration.

The power of this process can be demonstrated in a very simple manner. Place your mind in the psychological field, and then concentrate subjectively upon your hand, arousing at the time a deep desire for the increase of circulation in your hand. In a few moments, the veins on the back of your hand will be filled to capacity, and your hand, even though it might have been cold in the beginning, will become comfortably warm. Another experiment that is not only interesting in this connection, but may prove very valuable, is to concentrate in this same manner upon your digestive organs, in case the digestive process is retarded. You will soon feel more energy accumulating throughout the abdominal region, and any unpleasant sensation that you might have felt on account of indigestion will disappear entirely; in fact, even chronic indigestion can be cured in this way if the method is applied for a few minutes immediately before and after each meal. The idea is simply this, that when you give extra energy to an organ, it will be able to perform its function properly, and whenever any function is performed properly, any ailment that might have existed in the organ of that function, will disappear. A number of similar experiments may be tried, all of which will prove equally interesting, and besides, will train the mind to apply this great law of transmutation.

The following effects may be secured through transmutation: Working capacity in any part of the personality or mentality may be constantly increased; all the energy generated in the system may be employed practically and successfully; the mind may be made more brilliant, as it is an extraordinary amount of creative energy going into the mind that invariably causes mental brilliancy. Any faculty selected can be given so much of this surplus energy of the system, that it will almost from the beginning, manifest an increase in ability, and will, in the course of time, manifest rare talent and even genius. Moral purity may become second nature, as all that energy that was previously squandered in impure thought, impure desire or impure action can be transmuted readily, and applied in the building of a more vigorous personality and a more brilliant mind. A better control of all the forces of the personality may be obtained, and that mysterious something called personal magnetism may be acquired to a remarkable degree.

The attainment or accumulation of personal magnetism is something that we all desire, and the reason why is evident. What is called personal magnetism is the result of an extra amount of creative energy stored up in the personality and caused to circulate harmoniously throughout the personality. And the effect of this power is very marked. People who possess it are invariably more attractive, regardless of shape and form, and they are invariably more successful, no matter what their work may be. Hundreds of illustrations could be mentioned proving conclusively the extreme value of personal magnetism, though we are all so familiar with the fact that we do not require proof in the matter. What we want to know is what this power really is, how it may be produced, and why those who possess it have such a great advantage over those who do not possess it.

To illustrate, we may take two women who look alike in every respect; who have the same character and the same mentality, and who are equals in every respect but one, and that is that the one has personal magnetism while the other has not. But we need not be told of the fact. The woman who does not possess this power cannot be compared in any way with the woman who does possess it. The woman who does possess this power is far more attractive, far more brilliant, and seems to possess qualities of far greater worth; and the reason is that personal magnetism tends to heighten the effect of everything that you are, or that you may do. If we should compare two business men of equal ability and power, the one having personal magnetism and the other one not, we should find similar results. The one having this power would be far more successful, regardless of the fact that his ability and power in other respects were the same as his associate. Even men of ordinary ability succeed remarkably when they have personal magnetism; and we all know of women who are as plain as nature could make them, and yet being in possession of personal magnetism, are counted among the most attractive to be found anywhere. The most ordinary human form becomes a thing of beauty if made alive with this mysterious power, and a personality that had no attraction whatever, will fascinate everybody to a marked degree if charged with this power. We all know this to be true; we are therefore deeply interested to know how this power might be secured.

In the first place, we must remember that personal magnetism does not exercise its power by controlling or influencing other minds as many have sup posed. The fact is if you try to influcnce others, you will lose this power, and lose it completely no matter how strong it may be at the present time. The secret of personal magnetism simply lies in the fact that it tends to bring out into expression the best that is in you, and tends to heighten the effect of every expression; or, in other words, it causes every expression to act to the best advantage; though we find this power exercising its pecuuar effect not only in the personality and in the mentality of the individual, but also in his work.

When a musician has this power, his music charms to a far greater degree than if he does not possess it. There is something not only in the singing voice, but also in the speaking voice that indicates the absence or presence of this power. What it is no one can exactly describe, but we know it is there, and it adds immeasurably to the quality of what is expressed through the voice. In the field of literature we find the action of this power to be very marked. A writer who does not possess this mysterious force may write well, but there is something lacking in what he has written. On the other hand, if he has this power, he gives not only added charm to what he has written, but his ideas invariably appear to be more brilliant. In fact, there seems to be a power in everything he writes that is not ordinarily found on the printed page. On the stage this power is one of the principal factors, and we frequently find that the only difference between the good actor and a poor one, is the possession of a high degree of personal magnetism. No matter how well an actor may act, if he lacks in this power, he cannot succeed on the stage. When we go into the social world, we find the same fact. Those who possess this power are invariably the favourites, even though they may be lacking in many other qualities. In the business world we find in every case that a man who is lacking in personal magnetism is at a disadvantage, while the one who has an abundance of this power will have no difficulty, other things being equal, in working himself to the fore.

In a deeper study of this force, we find that it affects every movement of the body, every action of the mind, and every feeling or expression that mind and personality may produce; that is, it seems to give something additional to every action or movement, and makes everything about the individual more attractive. We might say that this force sets off everything about the person to a greater advantage. This power therefore does not act directly upon others, but acts directly upon the one who has it, and thereby makes the individual more striking, as well as more attractive, both in appearance and in conduct. What is good in you is made better if charged with this force, and every desirable effort that you may make produces a better effect in proportion. Added charm, added attractiveness and added efficiency— these invariably follow where the individual is in possession of a marked degree of this power. That which is beautiful is many times as beautiful where personal magnetism is in action, and that which is brilliant, becomes far more brilliant when combined with this mysterious force. Many people are born with it and apply it unconsciously, though the majority who have it, have acquired it through various forms of training. Any system of, exercise that tends to harmonize the movements of the body, will tend to increase to some extent the power of this force; though when such exercises are combined with the transmutation of creative energy, the results will be far greater. The reason for this is found in the fact that what is called personal magnetism is the result of a great deal of creative energy held in the system, or transmuted into harmonious muscular or mental activity.

The development of this power depends upon the proper training of the body in rhythmic movements, and the training of the surplus energy in the system to act harmoniously along the lines of constructive action in mind and body. A very important essential is to cultivate poise, which means peace and power combined. Try to feel deeply calm throughout your entire system, and at the same time, try to give full and positive action to every power in your system. Try to hold in your system all the energy generated, and the mere desire to do this will tend to bring about what may be called accumulation of energy. To experiment, try for several minutes to hold all your energy in your personality, and at the same time, try to give all of that energy harmonious action within your personality. In a few moments, you will actually feel alive with power, and if you have succeeded very well with your experiment, you will really feel like a storage battery for the time being. You will have so much energy that you will feel as if you could do almost anything. Experiment in this way at frequent intervals until you get your system into the habit of carrying out this process unconsciously. You will thereby cause your surplus energy to accumulate more and more in your system, and you will produce what may be called a highly charged condition of your personality, a condition that invariably means the attainment of personal magnetism. To secure this result, however, it is necessary to keep the mind in an undisturbed attitude, to avoid all bad habits, physical or mental, to be in harmony with everything and everybody, and to exercise full self-control under every circumstance.

In cultivating this power realize that it is the result of surplus energy held in the system, and caused to circulate harmoniously through every part of the system; remember that it is a power that does not act intentionally upon persons or circumstances; that its aim is not to control or influence anybody, but simply to act within the individual self, and heighten the effect of everything that he may be or do.

Never think or speak of that which you do not wish to happen.

The whine, the sting, and the sigh—these three must never appear in a single thought or a single word.

You can win ten times as many friends by talking happiness as you can by talking trouble. And the more real friends you have the less trouble you will have.

Speak well of everything good you find and mean it. When you find what you do not like keep quiet. The less you think or speak of what you do not like the more you have of what you do like.

Magnify the good; emphasize that which has worth; and talk only of those things that should live and grow.

When you have something good to say, say it. When you have something ill to say, say something else.

XVII
THE BUILDING POWER OF CONSTRUCTIVE SPEECH

THERE is a science of speech, and whoever wishes to promote his welfare and advancement must understand this science thoroughly and regulate his speech accordingly. Every word that is spoken exercises a power in personal life, and that power will work either for or against the person, depending upon the nature of the word. You can talk yourself into trouble, poverty or disease, and you can talk yourself into harmony, health and prosperity. In brief, you can talk yourself into almost any condition, desirable or undesirable.

Every word is an expression and every expression produces a tendency in some part of the system. This tendency may appear in the mind, in the body, in the chemical life of the body, in the world of desire, in character, among the various faculties, or anywhere in the personality, and will work itself out wherever it appears. Our expressions determine largely where we are to go, what we are to accomplish, and how we are to meet those conditions through which we may pass.

When our expressions produce tendencies towards sickness and failure, we will begin to move towards those conditions, and if the tendency is very strong, all the creative energies in the system will move in the same direction, focusing their efforts upon sickness and failure, or taking those conditions as their models, and thereby producing such conditions in the system. On the other hand, when our expressions produce tendencies towards health, happiness, power and success, we will begin to move towards those things, and in like manner create them in a measure.

Every word has an inner life force, sometimes called the hidden power of words, and it is the nature of this power that determines whether the expression is to be favourable or not. This power may be constructive or destructive. It may move towards the superior or the inferior. It may promote your purpose in life or it may retard that purpose, and it is the strongest when it is deeply felt. Therefore the words which we inwardly feel are the words that act as turning points in life. When you feel that trouble is coming, and express that feeling in your speech, you are actually turning in your path and are beginning to move towards that trouble. In addition you are creating troubled conditions in your system. We all know that the more trouble we feel in the midst of trouble, the more troublesome that trouble will become. And we also know that that that person who retains poise and self-control in the midst of trouble, will pass through it all without being seriously affected; and when it is over, is much wiser and stronger for the experience.

When you feel that better days are coming, and express that feeling in your speech, you turn all the power of your being towards the ideal of better days, and those powers will begin to create the better in your life. Whenever you talk about success, advancement, or any desirable condition, try to express the eeling of those things in your words. This inner feeling determines the tendencies of your creative powers; therefore, when you feel success in your speech, you cause the creative powers to create qualities in yourself that can produce success, while if you express the feeling of doubt, failure or loss in your words, those creative powers will produce inferiority, disturbance, discord, and a tendency to mistakes. It is in this way that the thing we fear comes upon us. Fear is a feeling that feels the coming of ills or other things we do not want; and as we always express through our words the feelings that we fear, we form tendencies toward those things, and the creative powers within us will produce them.

Whether the inner life force of a word will be constructive or destructive depends upon several factors, the most important of which are the tone, the motive and the idea. The tone of every word should be harmonious, wholesome, pleasing, and should convey a deep and serene expression. Words that express whines, discontent, sarcasm, aggressiveness and the like are destructive; so much so, that no one can afford to employ them under any circumstance whatever. Nothing is ever gained by complaints that are complaining, nor by criticisms that criticise. When things are not right, state so in a tone of voice that is firm and strong, but kind. A wronged customer who employs sweetness of tone as well as firmness of expression is one who will receive the first attention and the best attention, and nothing will be left unturned until the matter is set right.The words that wound others do far more injury to the person who gives them expression. No one therefore can afford to give expression to a single word that may tend to wound. Words of constructive power are always deeply felt. They are never loud or confusing, but always quiet and serene, filled with the very spirit of conviction.

Never give expression to what you do not wish to encourage. The more you talk about a thing the more you help it along. The "walls have ears" and the world is full of minds that will act upon your suggestion. Never mention the dark side of anything. It will interfere with your welfare. To tell your troubles may give you temporary relief, but it is scattering sited broadcast that will produce another crop of more trouble. If you have troubles, turn your back upon them and proceed to talk about harmony, freedom, attainment and success, and feel deeply the spirit of these new and better conditions. Thus you will begin to create for yourself a new life, new opportunities, new environment and a new world. Never speak unless you have something to say that gives cheer, encouragement, information or wholesome entertainment. To talk for the mere sake of talking is to throw precious energy away, and no human chatterbox will ever acquire greatness.

The motive back of every word should be constructive, and the life expressed in every word should convey the larger, the better, and the superior. Such words have building power, and are additions to life of extreme value. Every word should express, as far as possible, the absolute truth, and should never convey ideas that are simply indicated by appearances.

What is meant by speaking the absolute truth, however, is a matter that the majority do not understand, and as it is a very large subject, it would require pages to give even a brief scientific definition. But for practical purposes, the subject can be made sufficiently clear through the use of a few illustrations taken from the world's daily speech. People who think they have to say something and have nothing in particular to say, always take refuge in a brief description of the weather. In their descriptions they usually employ such expressions as "It is terribly hot," " it is an awful day," " This is terrible weather," "This is a miserably cold day," and so on. But such expressions do not change the weather, and there is no use of talking if your words are not to be of value in some way. You may say all sorts of disagreeable things about the weather without changing the weather in the least, but will such expressions leave you unchanged? Positively not ! Whenever you declare that something is horrible, you cause horrible thoughts to send their actions all through your nervous system. These actions may be weak, but many drops, no matter how small, will finally wear away a rock.

When people talk about themselves, they seldom fail to give expression to a score of detrimental statements. Here are a few: "I can't stand this," "I feel so tired,"

"I cannot bear to think of it," "I am thoroughly disgusted," "I am so susceptible to climatic changes," "I am so sensitive and so easily disturbed," "I am getting weak and nervous," "My memory is failing," "I am getting old," " I cannot work the way I used to," " My strength is gradually leaving me," "There is no chance for me any more," "Everything in life is uphill work," "I have passed a miserable night," " This has been a hard day," "I have nothing but trouble and bad luck," "You know I am human and so very weak," " There is always something wrong no matter how hard you try," "You know I have to be so very careful about what I eat as nearly everything disagrees with me."

A thousand other statements, all of them destructive, might be mentioned, but anyone who understands the power of thought will realize at once that such statements can never be otherwise but injurious and should therefore be avoided absolutely. But these statements are not only injurious—they are also untrue—absolutely untrue in every sense of the term.

The fact is you can stand almost anything if you forget your human weakness and array yourself in spiritual strength. You do not have to get tired. Work does not make anyone tired so long as he gets eight hours of sleep every night. It is wrong thinking that makes people tired. These are scientific facts. That person who permits himself to become disgusted at anything whatever is talking himself down to the plane of inferiority. When you feel disgusted you think disgusting thoughts, and such thoughts clog the mind. You cannot afford to think disgusting thoughts simply because something else is disgusting, because we daily become like the thoughts we think. We cannot improve disagreeable things by making ourselves disagreeable. Two wrongs never made a right. The proper course is to forgive the wrong-doer, forget the wrong and then do something substantial to right the whole matter. When we think kindly of the weather, place ourselves in harmony with Nature, think properly and dress properly, we shall not be susceptible to changes in the atmosphere; but so long as we say that we are affected by changing atmospheres, we not only make ourselves negative and susceptible, but we also produce detrimental effects in our systems through our own unwholesome beliefs. The man who constantly thinks he is easily disturbed disturbs himself. When we are in harmony with everything including ourselves and refuse to be otherwise, nothing will ever disturb us. That person who is nervous can make the matter worse by saying that he is nervous, because such a statement is a nervous statement and is full of discord. When we begin to feel nervous, we can remedy the matter absolutely by resolving to remain calm, and by employing only quiet, wholesome and constructive speech. Your words will cause you to move in the direction indicated by the nature of those words, and it is just as easy to use words that bring calmness and poise, as those that bring inharmony and confusion.

Modern science has demonstrated conclusively that there is nothing about a person that gets old. Therefore, to say that you are getting old is to persist in speaking the untruth, and it is but natural that you should reap as you sow. We must remember that a false appearance comes from the practice of judging from appearances. To state that your strength is failing is likewise to speak the untruth. There is but one strength in the universe—the strength of the Supreme—and that strength can never fail. You may have as much of that strength as you desire. All that is necessary for you to do is to live in perfect touch with the Supreme, and never think, do or say anything that will interfere with that sublime oneness. The strength of the Supreme is just as able to fill your system with life and power now as it was at any time in the past. Therefore, there is no real reason whatever why your power should diminish. Be true to the truth and your power will perpetually increase.

The belief that there are no opportunities for you is caused by the fact that you have hidden yourself in a cave of inferiority. Go out into the life of worth, ability and competence, and you will find more opportunities than you can use. The world is ever in search of competent minds, and modern knowledge has made it possible for man to develop his ability. No one therefore has any legitimate reason for speaking of hard luck or hard times unless he prefers to live in want. The more you complain about hard times, the harder times will become for you, while if you resolve to forget that there is such a thing as failure and proceed to make your own life as you wish it to be, the turn in the lane will surely come.

The idea that the pathway of life is all uphill work is also a false one, and if we give that idea expression we are simply placing obstacles in our way. Nothing is uphill work when we approach it properly, and there is nothing that helps more to place us in true relationship with things than true expression.

If the night has been unpleasant, never mention the fact for a moment. To talk about it will only produce more unpleasantness in your system. There is nothing wrong about the night. The unpleasantness was most likely produced by your own perverse appetite, or by some reckless inexcusable act. Forgive yourself and declare that you will never abuse nature any more. Such powerful words if repeated often, will turn the tendency of your habits, and your life will become natural and wholesome.

No day would be hard if we met all things with the conviction that we are equal to every occasion. Live properly, think properly, work properly and talk properly, and trouble and ill-luck will not trouble you seriously anymore. That person who declares that there is always something wrong is always doing something to make things wrong. When we have wrong on the brain we will make many mistakes, so there will always be something wrong brewing for us. When wrong things come, set them right and look upon the experience as an opportunity for you to develop greater mastership.

When you agree with yourself, all wholesome and properly prepared food will agree with you. But you cannot expect food to agree with you so long as you are disagreeable; and to declare that this or that always disagrees with you, is to fill your system with disagreeable thoughts, disturbed actions and conditions of discord. That nature can digest food under such circumstances no one can justly expect. There is nothing that injures digestion more than the habit of finding fault with the food. If you do not think that you can eat this or that, leave it alone, but leave it alone mentally as well as physically. it is not enough to drop a disagreeable thing from your hands; you must also drop it from your mind.

Remember, you are mentally living with everything that you talk about, and there is nothing that affects us more than that which we take into our mental life It is therefore not only necessary to speak the truth about all things, but also to avoid speaking about those things that are unwholesome. To speak about that which is wrong or inferior is never wholesome, no matter how closely we think we stand by the facts. Seeming facts, or what is called relative truth, should never receive expression unless they deal with that which is conducive to higher worth; and when circumstances compel us to make exceptions to this rule, we should avoid giving any feeling to what we say.

The greatest essential, however, is to make all speech constructive. Search for the real truth that is at the foundation of all life, and then give expression to such words as convey the full significance to that truth. The results, to say the least, will be extraordinary.

In daily conversation, the law of constructive speech should be most conscientiously applied. What we say to others will determine to a considerable degree what they are to think, and what tendencies their mental actions are to follow; and since man is the product of his thought, conversation becomes a most important factor in man.

We steadily grow into the likeness bf that which we think of the most, and what we are to think about depends largely upon the mode, the nature and the subject matter of our conversation. When conversation originates or intensifies the tendency to think about the wrong, the ordinary or the inferior, it becomes destructive, and likewise it tends to keep before mind the faults and defects that may exist in human nature. To be constructive, conversation should tend to turn attention upon the better side, the stronger side, the superior side of all things, and should give the ideal the most prominent place in thought, speech or expression. All conversation should be so formed that it may tend to move the mind towards the higher domains of thought, and should make everybody more keenly conscious of the greater possibilities that exist within them. No word should ever be spoken that will, in any way, bring the person's faults or short-comings before his mind, nor should any form of speech be permitted that may cause sadness, offence, depression or pain. Every word should convey hope, encouragement and sunshine.

To constantly remind a person of his faults is to cause him to become more keenly conscious of those faults. He will think more and more about his faults, and will thereby cause his faults to become more prominent and more troublesome than they ever were before. The more we think about our weakness, the weaker we become; and the more we talk about weakness, the more we think about weakness. Conversation therefore should never touch upon those things that we do not wish to retain or develop. The only way to remove weakness is to develop strength, and to develop strength we must keep attention constantly upon the quality of strength. We develop what we think about provided all thinking has depth, quality and continuity.

Conversation has exceptional value in the training of young minds, and in many instances may completely change the destinies of these minds. To properly train a child, his attention should be directed as much as possible upon those qualities that have worth and that are desired in his development; and the way he is spoken to will largely determine where he is to give the greater part of his attention. To scold a child is to remind him of his faults. Everytime he is reminded of his faults he gives more attention, more thought, and more strength to those faults. His good qualities are thereby made weaker while his bad qualities are made worse. It is not possibe to improve the mind and the character of the child by constantly telling him not to do " this" or " that." As a rule, it will increase his desire to do this other thing, and he will cease only through fear, or after having wasted a great deal of time in experiences that have become both disgusting and bitter.

It is the tendency of every mind to desire to do what it is told not to do, the reason being that negative commands are nearly always associated with fear; and when mind is in the attitude of fear, or dread or curiosity, it is very easily impressed by whatever it may be thinking about.

When we are warned we either enter a state of fear or one of curiosity, and while in those states, our minds are so deeply and so easily impressed by that from which we are warned, that we give it our whole attention. The result is we think so much about it that we become almost completely absorbed in it; and we are carried away, so to speak, not away from the danger, but into it.

When anyone is going wrong, it is a mistake to warn him not to go further. It is also a mistake to leave him alone. The proper course is to call his attention to somethmg better, and frame our conversation in such a way that he becomes wholly absorbed in the better. He will then forget his old mistakes, his old faults and his old desires, and will give all his life and power to the building of that better which has engaged his new interest.

The same law may be employed to prevent sickness and failure. When the mind becomes so completely absorbed in perfect health that all sickness is forgotten, all the powers of mind will proceed to create health, and every trace of sickness will soon disappear. When the mind becomes so completely absorbed in higher attainments and in greater achievements that all thought of failure is forgotten, all the forces of mind will begin to work for the promotion of those attainments and achievements. The person will be gaining ground every day, and greater success will positively follow.

To cause the mind to forget the wrong, the lesser and the inferior, constructive conversation may be employed with unfailing results; in fact, such conversation must be employed if the mind is to advance and develop. Our conversation must be in perfect accord with our ambitions, our desires, and our ideals, and all our expressions must aim to promote the real purpose we have in view.

It is the tendency of nearly every mind to try to make his friends perfect according to his own idea of perfection, and he usually proceeds by constantly talking to his friends about their faults, and what they should not do in order to become as perfect as his ideal. Parents, as a rule, do the same with their children, not knowing that through this method many are made worse; and it is only those who are very strong in mind and character that are not adversely affected by this method.

To help our friends or our children to become ideal, we should never mention their faults. Our conversation should deal with the strong points of character and the greater possibilities of mind. We should so frame our conversation that we tend to make everybody feel there is something in them. Our conversation should have an optimistic tendency and an ascending tone. It should deal with those things in life that are worthwhile, and it should always give the ideal the greatest prominence. Weaknesses of human nature should be recognized as little as possible, and should seldom, if ever, be mentioned. When people engage in destructive conversation in our midst we should try to change the subject, by calling their attention to the better side. There always is another and a better side; and when examined closely will be found to be far greater and infinitely more important than the ordinary side. Admirable qualities exist everywhere, and it will prove profitable to give these our undivided attention.

The first mark of a master mind is that he is able to promote his own perpetual improvement. The second is that he is able to be strong, joyous and serene under every circumstance.

The imagining faculty is the creative faculty of the mind, the faculty that creates plans, methods and ideas. Our imagination therefore must always be clear, lofty, wholesome, and constructive if we would create superior ideas and build for greater things.

Before you can have greater success you must become a greater man. Before you can become a greater man you must reach out toward the new and the greater along all lines; and this is possible only through the constructive use of imagination.

You get your best ideas when your mind acts in the upper story. And in all fields of action it is the best ideas that win.

THE BUDDHA

XVIII
IMAGINATION AND THE MASTER MIND

THE forces of the human system must have something definite to work for; that is, they must have an ideal upon which to concentrate their attention, or some model or pattern to follow as they proceed with their constructive actions.

To form this model, it is the power of imagination that must be employed, and that power must, in each case, be applied constructively. What we imagine becomes a pattern for the creative energies of mind and personality, and as the creations of these energies determine what we are to become and attain, we realize that the imaging faculty is one of the most important of all our faculties. We therefore cannot afford to lose a moment in learning how to apply it according to the laws of mental construction and growth.

To proceed, imagine yourself becoming and attaining what you wish to become and attain. This will give your energies a model, both of your greater future self and your greater future achievements. When you think of your future, always imagine success and greater things, and have no fear as to results. If you fear, you give your creative energies a model of failure, and they will accordingly proceed to create failure. Then we must also remember if we wish to succeed, our faculties must work successfully, but no faculty can work successfully when filled with fear. It is only when constantly inspired by the idea of success that any faculty or power in the human system can do its best.

To inspire our faculties with this idea, we should always imagine ourselves obtaining success. The picture of success should be placed upon all the walls of the mind, so that the powers within us will see success, and success only as their goal. Hang up pictures in your mind that will inspire you to do your best; hang up pictures in your mind that will cause you to think constantly of that which you desire to accomplish, and this you may do by imagining yourself being that greater something that you want to be and doing that greater something that you want to do.

An excellent practice is to use your spare moments in creating such pictures in your imagination and placing them in the most conspicuous position of your mind, so that all your faculties and powers can see them at all times. We are always imagining something. It is practically impossible to be awake without imagining something. Then why not imagine something at all times that will inspire the powers within us to do greater and greater things?

To aid the imagination in picturing the greater, the higher and better, we should "hitch our wagon to a star." The star may be something quite out of reach as far as present circumstances indicate, but if we hitch our wagon to something in such a lofty position, our mind will begin to take wings. It will no longer be like a worm crawling in the dust. We shall begin to rise and continue to rise.

The only thing that can cause the mind to rise is imagination. The only thing that can make the mind larger than it is, is imagination. The only thing that can make the mind act along new lines is imagination. This being true, it is unwise to use the imagination for any other purpose than for the best that we can think or do.

In this connection, there are a few suggestions that will be found of special value. First, make up your mind as to what you really want in every respect. Determine what surroundings or environment you want. Decide upon the kind of friends you want and what kind of work you would prefer. Make all those ideals so good and so perfect that you will have no occasion to change them. Then fix those ideals so clearly in mind that you can see them at all times, and proceed to desire their realization with all the power of mind and soul. Make that your frrst step.

Your second step should be to imagine yourself living in those surroundings that you have selected as your ideal; then make it a point to live in that imagination every moment of every day. Instead of imagining a number of useless things during spare moments, as people usually do, imagine yourself living in those surroundings and those ideals. Imagine yourself in the presence of friends that are exactly what you wish your ideal friends to be, and permit your fancy to run as far as it may wish along all of those idealistic lines. If you have not found your work, proceed to imagine yourself doing what you wish to do. If you have already found your work, imagine yourself doing that work as well as you would wish, and imagine the coming of results as large as your greatest desires could expect. Devote every moment of your spare time to the placing of those ideals before your attention, and you will give your power and forces something strong and definite to work for. Every mental force is an artist, and it paints according to the model. What you imagine is the model, and there is not a single mental action that is not inspired or called forth into action by some picture or model which the imagination has produced.

The imagination can call forth the ordinary or the extraordinary. It can give the powers of your being an inferior model or an extraordinary model, and if the imagination is not directed to produce the extraordinary and the superior, it is quite likely to produce the ordinary and the inferior. Your second step, therefore, should be to imagine yourself actually living in those surroundings that you have selected as your ideal, and in actually becoming and doing what you are determined to become and do.

This practice would, in the first place, give you a great deal of pleasure, because if you have definite ideals and imagine yourself attaining those ideals, you will certainly enjoy yourself to a marked degree for the time being. But in addition to that enjoyment, you will gradually and steadily be training your mind to work for those greater things. The mind will work for that which is upper most in thought and imagination. Therefore, we should invariably place our highest ideals uppermost, so that the whole of our attention may be concentrated upon those ideals, and all the powers of our mind and personality directed to work for those ideals.

Your third step should be to proceed to apply the power of desire, the power of will, the power of scientific thought, and in brief, all your powers, in trying to realize those beautiful ideals that you continue to imagine as your own. Do as the ancient Hebrews did. First make your prediction. Then go to work and make it come true. What you imagine concerning your greater future is your prediction, and you can cause that prediction to come true if you apply all the power in your possession in working for its realization every day

The constructive use of imagination therefore will enable you to place a definite model or pattern before the forces of your system, so that those forces may have something better and greater to work for. In brief, instead of permitting most of your energies to go to waste and the remainder to follow any pattern or idea that may be suggested by your environment, or your own helterskelter thinking you will cause all your energy to work for the greatest and the best that you may desire.

This is the first use of imagination, and it easily places this remarkable faculty among the greatest in the human mind. Another use of the imagination is found in its power to give the mind something definite to think about at all times, so that the mind may be trained to always think of that which you really want to think; that is, through this use of the imagination, you can select your own thought and think your own thought at all times; and he who can do this is gradually becoming a master mind.

The master mind is the mind that thinks what it wants to think, regardless of what circumstances, environment or associations may suggest. The mind that masters itself creates its own ideas, thoughts and desires through the original use of imagination, or its own imaging faculty. The mind that does not master itself forms its thoughts and desires after the likeness of the impressions received through the senses, and is therefore controlled by those conditions from which, such impressions come; because as we think, so we act and live. The average mind usually desires what the world desires without any definite thought as to his own highest welfare or greatest need, the reason being that a strong tendency to do likewise is always produced in the mind when the desires are formed in the likeness of such impressions as are suggested by external conditions. It is therefore evident that the person who permits himself to be affected by suggestions will invariably form artificial desires; and to follow such desires is to be misled.

The master mind desires only that which is conducive to real life and in the selection of its desires is never influenced in the least by the desires of the world. Desire is one of the greatest powers in human life. It is therefore highly important that every desire be normal and created for the welfare of the individual himself. But no desire can be wholly normal that is formed through the influence of suggestion. Such desires are always abnormal to some degree, and easily cause the individual to be misplaced.

A great many people are misplaced. They do not occupy those places wherein they may be their best and accomplish the most. They are working at a disadvantage, and are living a life that is far inferior to what they are intended to live. The cause is frequently found in abnormal or artificial desires. They have imitated the desires of others without consulting their present needs. They have formed the desire to do what others are doing by permitting their minds to be influenced by suggestions and impressions from the world, forgetting what their present state of development makes them capable of doing now. By imitating the lives, habits, actions and desires of others, they are led into a life not their own; that is, they are misplaced.

The master mind is never misplaced because he does not live to do what others are doing, but what he himself wants to do now. He wants to do only that which is conducive to real life, a life worthwhile, a life that steadily works up to the very highest goal in view.

The average mind requires a change of environment before he can change his thought. He has to go somewhere or bring into his presence something that will suggest a new line of thinking and feeling. The master mind, however, can change his thought whenever he so desires. A change of scene is not necessary, because such a mind is not controlled from without. A change of scene will not produce a change of thought in the master mind unless he so elects. The master mind changes his thoughts, ideals or desires by imaging upon the mind the exact likeness of the new ideas, the new thoughts, and the new desires that have been selected.

The secret of the master mind is found wholly in the intelligent use of imagination. Man is as he thinks, and his thoughts are patterned after the predominating mental images, whether those images are impressions suggested from without, or impressions formed by the ego acting from within. When man permits his thoughts and desires to be formed in the likeness of impressions received from without, he will be more or less controlled by environment and he will be in the hands of fate, but when he transforms every impression received from without into an original idea and incorporates that idea into a new mental image, he uses environment as a servant, thereby placing fate in his own hands.

Every object that is seen will produce an impression upon the mind according to the degree of susceptibility. This impression will contain the nature of the object of which it is a representation. The nature of this object will be reproduced in the mind, and what has entered the mind will be expressed more or less throughout the entire system. Therefore, the mind that is susceptible to suggestions will reproduce in his own mind and system conditions that are similar in nature to almost everything that he may see, hear or feel. He will consequently be a reflection of the world in which he lives. He will think, speak and act as that world may suggest; he will float with the stream of that world wherever that stream may flow; he will not be an original character, but an automaton.

Every person that permits himself to be affected by suggestion is more or less an automaton, and is more or less in the hands of fate. To place fate in his own hands, he must use suggestions intelligently instead of blindly following those desires and thoughts that his surroundings may suggest. We are surrounded constantly by suggestions of all kinds, because everything has the power to suggest something to that mind that is susceptible, and we are all more or less susceptible in this respect. But there is a vast difference between permitting oneself to be susceptible to suggestion and training oneself to intelligently use those impressions that suggestions may convey.

The average writer on suggestion not only ignores this difference, but encourages susceptibility to suggestion by impressing the reader with the remark that suggestion does control the world. If it is true that suggestion controls the world, more or less, we want to learn how to so use suggestion that its control of the human mind will decrease steadily; and this we can accomplish, not by teaching people how to use suggestion for the influencing of other minds, but in using those impressions conveyed by suggestion in the reconstruction of their own minds. Suggestion is a part of life, because everything has the power to suggest, and all minds are open to impressions. Nothing therefore can be said against suggestion by itself. Suggestion is a factor in our midst; it is a necessary factor. The problem is to train ourselves to make intelligent use of the impressions received, instead of blindly following the desires produced by those impressions as the majority do.

To proceed in the solution of this problem, never permit objects discerned by the senses to reproduce themselves in your mind against your will. Form your own ideas about what you see, hear or feel, and try to make those ideas superior to what was suggested by the objects discerned. When you see evil do not form ideas that are in the likeness of that evil; do not think of the evil as bad, but try to understand the forces that are back of that evil—forces that are good in themselves though misdirected in their present state. By trying to understand the nature of the power that is back of evil or adversity, you will not form bad ideas, and therefore will feel no bad effects from experiences that may seem undesirable. At the same time, you will think your own thought about the experiences, thereby developing the power of the master mind.

Surround yourself as far as possible with those things that suggest the superior, but do not permit such suggestions to determine your thought about the superior. Those superior impressions that are suggested by superior environment should be used in forming still more superior thoughts. If you wish to be a master mind, your thought must always be higher than the thought your environment may suggest, no matter how ideal that environment may be. Every impression that enters the mind through the senses should be worked out and should be made to serve the mind in its fullest capacity. In this way the original impression will not reproduce itself in the mind, but will become instrumental in giving the mind a number of new and superior ideas.

To work out an impression, try to see through its whole nature. Look at it from every conceivable point of view, and try to discern its actions, tendencies, possibilities and probable defects. Use your imagination in determining what you want to think or do, what you are to desire and what your tendencies are to be. Know what you want, and then image those things upon the mind constantly. This will develop the power to think what you want to think, and he who can think what he wants to think is on the way to becoming what he wants to become.

The principal reason why the average person does not realize his ideals is because he has not learned to think what he wants to think. He is too much affected by the suggestions that are about him. He imitates the world too much, following desires that are not his own. He is therefore misled and misplaced. Whenever you permit yourself to think what persons, things, conditions or circumstances may suggest, you are not following what you yourself want to think. You are not following your own desires but borrowed desires. You will therefore drift into strange thinking, and thinking that is entirely different from what you originally planned. To obey the call of every suggestion and permit your mind to be carried away by this, that or the other, will develop the tendency to drift until your mind will wander. Concentration will be almost absent and you will become wholly incapable of actually thinking what you want to think. One line of constructive thinking will scarcely be begun when another line will be suggested, and you will leave the unfinished task to begin something else, which in turn will be left incomplete. Nothing, therefore, will be accomplished.

To become a master mind, think what you want to think, no matter what your surroundings may suggest; and continue to think what you want to think until that particular line of thought or action has been completed. Desire what you want to desire and impress that desire so deeply upon consciousness that it cannot possibly be disturbed by those foreign desires that environment may suggest; and continue to express that desire with all the life and power that is in you until you get what you want. When you know that you are in the right desire, do not permit anything to influence your mind to change. Take such suggestions and convert them into the desire you have already decided upon, thereby giving that desire additional life and power. Never close your mind to impressions from without. Keep the mind open to the actions of all those worlds that may exist in your sphere and try to gain valuable impressions from every source, but do not blindly follow those impressions. Use them constructively in building up your own system of original thought. Think what you want to think, and so use every impression you receive that you gain greater power to think what you want to think. Thus you will gradually become a master mind.

Follow the vision of the soul. Be true to your ideals no matter what may happen now. Then things will take a turn and the very things you wanted to happen will happen.

The ideal has a positive drawing power towards the higher, the greater, and the superior. Whoever gives his attention constantly to the ideal, therefore, will steadily rise in the scale.

Take things as they are today and proceed at once to make them better.

Expect every change to lead you to something better and it will. As your faith is so shall it be.

To be human as not to be weak. To be human is to be all that there is in man, and the greatness that as contained in the whole of man is marvellous indeed.

XIX
THE HIGHER FORCES IN MAN

I T is the most powerful among the forces of the human system that we least understand, and though this may seem unfortunate, it is not unnatural. All advancement is in the ascending scale. We learn the simplest things first and the least valuable in the beginning. Later on, we learn that which is more important. We find therefore the greatest forces among those that are almost entirely hidden, and for that reason they are sometimes called the hidden forces, the finer forces, or the higher forces.

As it is in man, so it is also in nature. We find the most powerful among natural forces to be practically beyond comprehension. Electricity is an illustration. There is no greater force known in nature, and yet no one has thus far been able to determine what this force actually is. The same is true with regard to other natural forces; the greater they are and the more powerful they are, the more difficult it is to understand them. In the human system, there are a number of forces of exceptional value that we know nothing about; that is, we do not understand their real nature, but we can learn enough about the action, the purpose and the possibilities of those forces to apply them to practical life; and it is practical application with which we are most concerned.

The field of the finer forces in mind may be termed the unconscious mental field, and the vastness of this field, as well as the possibilities of its functions, is realized when we learn that the greater part of our mental world is unconscious. Only a fraction of the mental world of man is on the surface or up in consciousness; the larger part is submerged in the depths of what might be called a mental sea of subconsciousness. All modern psychologists have come to this conclusion, and it is a fact that anyone can demonstrate in his own experience if he will take the time.

In the conscious field of the human mind, we fmd those actions of which we are aware during what may be called our wide-awake state; and they are seemingly insignificant in comparison with the actions of the vast unconscious world, though our conscious actions are found to be highly important when we learn that it is the conscious actions that originate unconscious actions. And here let us remember that it is our unconscious actions that determine our own natures, our own capabilities, as well as our own destiny. In our awakened state we continue to think and act in a small mental field, but all of those actions are constantly having their effect upon this vast unconscious field that is found beneath the mental surface.

To realize the existence of this unconscious mental world, and to realize our power to determine the actions of that world, is to awaken within us a feeling that we are many times as great and as capable as we thought we were, and the more we think of this important fact, the larger becomes our conscious view of life and its possibilities.

To illustrate the importance of the unconscious field and your finer forces, we will take the force of love. No one understands the nature of this force, nor has anyone been able to discover its real origin or its actual possibilities; nevertheless, it is a force that is tremendously important in human life. Its actions are practically hidden, and we do not know what constitutes the inner nature of those actions, but we do know how to control those actions in a measure for our own good; and we have discovered that when we do control and properly direct the actions of love, its value to everybody concerned is multiplied many times. It is the same with a number of other forces with which we are familiar. They act along higher or finer lines of human consciousness, and they are so far beyond ordinary comprehension that we cannot positively know what they are, but we do know enough about them to control them and direct them for our best and greatest good. In like manner, the unconscious mental field, though beyond scientific analysis, is sufficiently understood as to its modes of action, so that we can control and direct those actions as we may choose. When we analyse what comes forth from the unconscious field at any time, we find that it is invariably the result of something that we caused to be placed in that field during some past time. This leads up to the discovery of unconscious mental processes, and it is not difficult to prove the existence of such processes.

Many a time ideas, desires, feelings or aspirations come to the surface of thought that we are not aware of having created at any time. We come to the conclusion, therefore, that they were produced by some unconscious process, but when we examine those ideas or desires carefully, we find that they are simply effects corresponding exactly with certain causes that we previously placed in action in our conscious world. When we experiment along this line we find that we can produce a conscious process at any time, and through deep feeling cause it to enter the unconscious mental world. In that deeper world, it goes to work and produces according to its nature, the results coming back to the surface of our conscious mentality days, weeks or months later. The correspondence between conscious and unconscious mental processes may be illustrated by a simple movement in physical action. If a physical movement began at a certain point, and was caused to act with a circular tendency, it would finally come back to its starting point. It is the same with every conscious action that is deeply felt. It goes out into the vastness of the unconscious mental field, and having a circular tendency, as all mental actions have, it finally comes back to the point where it began; and in coming back, brings with it the result of every unconscious experience through which it passed on its circular journey.

To go into this subject deeply, and analyse every phase of it would be extremely interesting; in fact, it would be more interesting than fiction. It would require, however, a large book to do it justice. For this reason, we can simply touch upon the practical side of it, but will aim to make this brief outline sufficiently clear to enable anyone to direct his unconscious process in such a way as to secure the best results.

Every mental process, or every mental action, that takes place in our wide-awake consciousness will, if it has depth of feeling or intensity, enter the unconscious field, and after it has developed itself according to the line of its original nature, will return to the conscious side of the mind. Here we find the secret of character building, and also the secret of building faculties and talents. Everything that is done in the conscious field to improve the mind, character, conduct or thought will, if it has sincerity and depth of feeling, enter the unconscious field; and later will come back with fully developed qualities, which when in expression, constitutes character. Many a man, however, after trying for some time to improve himself and seeing no results, becomes discouraged. He forgets that some time always intervenes between the period of sowing and the period of reaping. What he does in the conscious field to improve himself, constitutes the sowing, when those actions enter the conscious field to be developed: and when they come back, it may be weeks or months later, the reaping time has arrived. Many a time, after an individual has given up self-improvement, he discovers, after a considerable period, that good qualities are beginning to come to the surface in his nature, thereby proving con-lusively that what he did months ago along that line was not in vain. The results of past efforts are beginning to appear. We have all had similar experiences, and if we would carefully analyse such experiences, we would find that not a single conscious process that is sufticiently deep or intense to become an unconscious process will fail to come back finally with its natural results. Many a time ideas come into our minds that we wanted weeks ago, and could not get them at that time; but we did place in action certain deep, strong desires for those ideas, at that particular time, and though our minds were not prepared to develop those ideas at once, they finally were developed and came to the surface.

The fact that this process never fails indicates the value of giving the mind something to work out for future need. If we have something that we want to do months ahead, we should give the mind definite instruction now and make those instructions so deep, that they will become unconscious processes. Those unconscious processes will, according to directions, work out the ideas and plans that we want for that future work, and in the course of time, will bring results to the surface. To go into detail along the line of this part of our study would also be more interesting than fiction, but again, a large book would be required to do it justice. However, if we make it a practice to place in action our best thoughts, our best ideas and our best desires now and every moment of the eternal now, we will be giving the unconscious mental field something good to work for at all times; and as soon as each product is finished, or ready to be delivered from the unconscious world, it will come to the surface, and will enter the conscious mind ready for use.

Some of the best books that have been written have been worked out during months of unconscious mental processes; the same is true with regard to inventions, dramas, musical compositions, business plans, and in fact, anything and everything of importance that could be mentioned. Every idea, every thought, every feeling, every desire, every mental action, may, under certain circumstances, produce an unconscious process corresponding with itself, and this process will in every instance bring back to consciousness the result of its work. When we realize this, and realize the vast possibilities of the unconscious field, we will see the advantage of placing in action as many good unconscious processes as possible. Give your unconscious mental world something important to do every hour. Place a new seed in that field every minute. It may take weeks or months before that seed brings forth its fruit, but it will bring forth, after its kind, in due time without fail.

We understand therefore, how we can build character by sowing seeds of character in this field, and how we can, in the same way, build desirable conduct, a different disposition, different mental tendencies, stronger and greater mental faculties, and more perfect talents along any line. To direct these unconscious processes, it is necessary to apply the finer forces of the system, as it is those forces that invariably determine how those processes are to act. Those forces, however, are very easily applied, as all that is necessary in the beginning is to give attention to the way we feel. The way we feel determines largely what our finer forces are to be and how they are to act, and there is not an hour when we do not feel certain energies at work in our system. All the finer forces are controlled by feeling. Try to feel what you want done either in the conscious or the unconscious mental fields, and you will place in action forces that correspond to what you want done. Those forces will enter the unconscious mental world and produce processes through which the desired results will be created.

Whenever you want to redirect any force that is highly refined, you must feel the way you want that force to act. To illustrate, we will suppose you have certain emotions in your mental world that are not agreeable. To give the energies of those emotions a new and more desirable force of action, change your emotions by giving your whole attention in trying to feel such emotions as you may desire. And here let us remember that every emotion that comes up in the system is teeming with energy; but as most emotions continue to act without any definite control, we realize how much energy is wasted through uncurbed emotions. We know from experience, that whenever we give way to our feelings, we become weak. The reason is that uncontrolled feeling wastes energy. A great many people who are very intense in their feelings, actually become sick whenever they give way to strong or deep emotions. On the other hand, emotions that are controlled and properly directed, not only prevent waste, but will actually increase the strength of mind and body. Here is a good practice. Whenever you feel the way you do not wish to feel, begin to think deeply and in the most interesting manner possible, of those things that you wish to accomplish. If you can throw your whole soul, so to speak, into those new directions, you will soon find your undesired feelings disappearing completely. Every individual should train himself to feel the way he wants to feel, and this is possible if he will always direct his attention to something desirable whenever undesired feelings come up. Through this practice he will soon get such full control over his feelings that he can always feel the way he wants to feel, no matter what the circumstances may be. He will thus gain the power not only of controlling his emotions and using constructively all those energies that invariably appear in his emotions, but he will also have found the secret of continued happiness. Whenever mental energy moves in a certain direction, it tends to build up power for good along that line. We realize therefore the value of directing all our attention upon those things in mind, character and life that we wish to build and develop.

In building character we find the results to be accumulative; that is, we make an effort to improve our life or conduct, and thereby produce an unconscious process, which will later on, give us more strength of character to be and live the way we wish to be and live. This in turn will enable us to produce more and stronger unconscious processes along the line of character building, which will finally return with a greater number of good qualities. The result of this action will be to give us more power to build for a still greater character, and so this process may be continued indefinitely.

The same is true with regard to building the mind. The more you build the mind, the greater becomes your mental power to build a still greater mind: but in each case, it is the unconscious process that must be produced in order that the greater character or greater mind may be developed from within. In this connection, it is well to remember that the principal reason why so many people fail to improve along any line is because their desires or efforts for improvement are not sufficiently deep and strong to become unconscious processes. To illustrate, it is like placing seed on stony ground. If the seed is not placed in good, deep soil it will not grow. You may desire self-improvement for days, but if those desires are weak or superficial, they will not enter the unconscious field; and any action however good it may be, if it fails to enter the unconscious field, will also fail to produce results along the line of self-improvement.

118

With regard to the building of character, we must also remember that character determines in a large measure the line of action of all the other forces in the human system. If your character is strong and well developed, every force that you place in action will be constructive; while if your character is weak, practically all your forces will go astray. This is not true in the moral field alone, but also in the field of mental achievement. If the character is weak, your ability will be mostly misdirected no matter how hard you may work, or how sincere you may be in your effort to do your best. This explains why a great many people do not realize their ideals. They have paid no attention to character building, and therefore, nearly every effort that they may have made in trying to work up towards their ideals, has been misdirected and sent astray. Whatever our ideals may be therefore, or how great our desires may be to realize those ideals, we must first have character; and even though we may be able to place in action the most powerful forces in the human system, we will not get results until we have character. It is character alone that can give the powers of man constructive direction, and it is a well known fact that those people who have a strong, firm, well-developed character easily move from the good to the better, no matter what the circumstances.

What may be called the higher forces in man act invariably through our most sublime states of consciousness, and as it is these higher forces that enable man to become or accomplish more than the average, it is highly important that we attain the power to enter sublime consciousness at frequent intervals. No man or woman of any worth was ever known, who did not have experience in these sublime states; in fact, it is impossible to rise above the ordinary in life or achievement without drawing, more or less, upon the higher realms of consciousness. People are sometimes criticized for not being on the earth all the time, but it is necessary to get above the earth occasionally in order to find something worthwhile to live for and work for while upon earth. The most powerful forces in human life can be drawn down to earth for practical use, but to get them we must go to the heights frequently. No one can write music unless his consciousness touches the sublime. No one can write real poetry unless he has the same experience. No one can evolve ideas worthwhile unless his mind transcends the so-called practical sphere of action, and no individual can rise in the world of attainment and achievement unless his mind dwells almost constantly on the verge of the sublime. Examine the minds of people of real worth, people who have something in them, people who are beyond the average, people who are rising in the scale, people whom we truly admire, people that we look up to, people who occupy high positions—positions that they have actually won through merit—and we find in every instance, that their minds touch frequently the sublime state of consciousness. When we touch that state, our minds are drawn up above the ordinary, and mental actions are developed and worked out that are superior to ordinary or average mental actions. It is therefore simply understood that experience in sublime consciousness if properly employed, will invariably make man greater and better.

When we look upon a man that we can truthfully say is a real man, we find that something unusual has been or is being expressed in his personality; and that something unusual is hidden in every personality. It is a hidden power, a hidden force, which, when placed in action, gives man superior worth, both as to character, ability and life. Real men and real women, people who are real in the true sense of the term, are always born from the sublime state of consciousness; that is, they have, through coming in contact with higher regions of thought, evolved greater worth in their own minds and personalities; and as this possibility is within reach of every man or woman, we see the importance of dealing thoroughly with these higher powers in human nature.

Whenever we touch those finer states in the upper regions of the mind, we invariably feel that we have gained something superior, something that we did not possess before; and the gaining of that something invariably makes life stronger as well as finer. The ordinary has been, in a measure, overcome, and that which is beyond the ordinary is being gradually evolved. If we would rise in the scale in the fullest and best sense of the term, we must pay close attention to those higher forces and make it a practice to enter frequently into close touch with higher states of consciousness; in fact, we simply must do it, because if we do not we will continue to move along a very ordinary level. Then we must also bear in mind that it is our purpose to use all the forces we possess, not simply those that we can discern on the outside or that we are aware of in external cosciousness, but also those finer and more powerful forces which we can control and direct only when we ascend to the heights.

In dealing with these greater powers in man, it will be worth our while to reconsider briefly the psychological field. As long as the mind acts on the surface of consciousness, we have very little control of those finer elements in human life, but when the mind goes into the depths of feeling, into the depths of realization, or into what is called the psychological field, then it is that it touches everything that has real worth or that has the power to evolve, produce or develop still greater worth. It is the active forces of the psychological field that determine everything that is to take place in the life of man, both within himself and in his external destiny. We must therefore learn to act through the psychological field if we would master ourselves and create our own future.

The psychological field can be defined as that field of subconscious action that permeates the entire personality, or that fills, so to speak, every atom of the physical man on a finer plane. The psychological field is a finer field, permeating the ordinary tangible physical elements of life, and we enter this field whenever our feelings are deep and sincere. The fact that the psychological field determines real worth, as well as the attainment of greater worth, is easily demonstrated in everyday experience. When a man has anything in him, his nature is always deep. The same is true of people of refinement or culture: there is depth to their natures, and the man of character invariably lives in that greater world of life and power that is back of, or beneath, the surface of consciousness. If there is something in you, you both live and act through the deeper realms of your life, and those realms constitute the psychological field.

Among the many important forces coming directly through emotion or feeling, one of the most valuable is that of enthusiasm. In the average mind, enthusiasm runs wild, but we have found that when this force is properly directed it becomes a great constructive power. When you are enthusiastic about something, it is always about something new or something better—something that holds possibilities that you did not realize before. Your enthusiasm, if properly directed, will naturally cause your mind to move towards those possibilities, and enthusiasm is readily directed when you concentrate attention exlusively upon that something new that inspires enthusiasm. By turning your attention upon the thing that produces enthusiasm, the mind will move forward toward those greater possibilities that are discerned. This forward movement of the mind will tend to renew and enlarge the mind so that it will gain a still greater conception of those possibilities. This will increase your enthusiasm, which will in turn impel your mind to move forward still further in the same direction. Thus a still larger conception of those possibilities will be secured, which in turn will increase your enthusiasm and the power of your mind to take a third step in advance. We thus realize that if enthusiasm is directed upon the possibilities that originally inspired that enthusiasm, we will not only continue to be enthused, but we will in that very manner, cause the mind to move forward steadily and develop steadily, so that in time it will gain sufficient power to actually work out those possibilities upon which attention has been directed. In this connection, we must also remember that we can grow and advance only as we pass into the new. It is new life, new thought, new states of consciousness that are demanded if we are to take any steps at all in advance, and as enthusiasm tends directly to inspire the mind to move towards the new, we see how important it is to continue, not only to live in the spirit of enthusiasm, but to direct that spirit upon the goal in view. It is invariably the enthusiastic mind that moves forward, that does things, and that secures results.

Two other forces of great value, belonging to this group, are appreciation and gratitude. Whenever you appreciate a certain thing you become conscious of its real quality, and whenever you become conscious of the quality of anything, you begin to develop that quality in yourself. When we appreciate the worth of a person, we tend to impress the idea of that worth in our own minds, and thereby cause the same effect to be produced, in a measure, in ourselves. The same is true if we appreciate our own worth, in a sensible and constructive manner. If we appreciate what we already are, and are ambitious to become still more, we focus our minds upon the greater, and employ what we already possess as stepping-stones towards the greater attainment; but when we do not appreciate ourselves, there are no stepping stones that we can use in attaining greater things. We thus realize why people that do not appreciate themselves never accomplish much, and why they finally go downgrade in nearly every instance.

When we appreciate the beautiful in anything, we awaken our minds to a higher and better understanding of the beautiful. Our minds thus become, in a measure, more beautiful. The same is true with regard to any quality. Whatever we appreciate, we tend to develop in ourselves, and here we find a remarkable aid to the power of concentration, because we always concentrate attention perfectly, naturally and thoroughly upon those things that we fully appreciate. Thus we understand why it is that we tend to develop in ourselves the things that we admire in others.

Whenever you feel grateful for anything, you always feel nearer to the real quality of that particular thing. A person who is ungrateful, however, always feels that there is a wall between himself and the good things in life. Usually there is such a wall, though he has produced it himself through his ingratiude. But the man who is grateful for everything, places himself in that attitude where he may come in closer contact with the best thing; everywhere; and we know very well that the most grateful people always receive the best attention everywhere. We all may meet disappointment at some time and not get exactly what we wanted, but we shall find that the more grateful we are, the less numerous will those disappointments become. It has been well said that no one feels inclined to give his best attention to the man who is always "knocking," and it is literally true. On the other hand, if you are really grateful and mean it, it is very seldom that you do not receive the best attention from everybody wherever you may go.

The most important side of this law, however, is found in the fact that the more grateful you are for everything good that comes into your life, the more closely you place your mind in contact with that power in life that can produce greater good.

Another among the finer forces is that of aspiration. No person should fail to aspire constantly and aspire to the very highest that he can possibly awaken in his life. Aspiration always tends to elevate the mind and tends to lift the mind into larger and greater fields of action. And when the mind finds itself in this larger field of action, it will naturally gain power to do greater things. We all realize that so long as we live down in the lower story, we can not accomplish very much; it is when we lift our minds to the higher stories of the human structure that we begin to gain possession of ideas and powers through which greater things may be achieved.

The same is true of ambition. Ambition not only tends to draw the mind up into higher and larger fields, but also tends to build up those faculties through which we are to work. If you are tremendously ambitious to do a certain thing, the force of that ambition will tend to increase the power and ability of that faculty through which your ambition may be realized. To illustrate, if you are ambitious to succeed in the business world, the force of that ambition if very strong, will constantly make your business faculties stronger and more able, so that finally your business ability will have become sufliciently great to carry your ambition through. You cannot be too ambitious, provided you are ambitious for something definite and continue to give your whole life and soul to that which you expect or desire to accomplish through that ambition. When we know the power of ambition, and know that anybody can be ambitious, we realize that anyone can move forward. No matter what his position may be, or where he may be, he can, through the power of ambition begin to gain ground, and continue to gain ground indefinitely. The average mind, however, has very little ambition, and makes no effort to arouse this tremendous force; but we may depend upon the fact that when this force is fully aroused in any mind, a change for the better must positively come before long.

The force of an ideal is another among the finer forces that should receive constant and thorough attention. When you have an ideal and live for it every second of your existence, you place yourself in the hands of a drawing power that is immense, and that power will tend to draw out into action every force, power and faculty that you may possess, especially those forces and qualities that will have to be developed in order that you may realize that ideal.

Have an ideal, and the highest that you can picture. Then worship it every hour with your whole soul. Never come down, and do not neglect it for a moment. We all know very well that it is the people who actually worship their high ideals with mind and heart and soul that finally realize those ideals. It is such people who reach the high places and the reason why is easily explained. Give your attention, or rather, your whole life to some lofty ideal, and you will tend to draw into action all the finer and higher forces of your system—those forces that can create greater ability, greater talent, greater genius—those forces that can increase your capacity, bring into action all your finer elements and give you superior power and superior worth in every sense of the term—those forces which, when aroused, cannot positively fail to do the work you wish to have done.

A fact well known in this connection is that when the mind is turned persistently upon a certain ideal, every power that is in you begins to flow in that direction, and this is the very thing you want. When we can get all that is in us to work for our ideals and to work towards our ideals, then we shall positively reach whatever goal we have in view.

Closely connected with our ideals, we find our visions and dreams. The man without a vision will never be anything but an ordinary man, and the people who never dream of greater things, will never get beyond ordinary things. It is our visions and dreams that lift our minds to lofty realms, that make us feel that there is something greater and better to work for; and when we become inspired with a desire to work for greater and better things, we will not only proceed to carry out those desires, but will finally secure suffrcient power to fulfil those desires. "The nation that has no vision shall perish." This is a great truth that we have heard a thousand times, and we know the reason why; but the same truth is applicable to man. If he has no vision, he will go down; but if he has visions, the highest and most perfect visions he can possibly imagine, and lives constantly for their realization, he will positively ascend in the scale. He will become a greater and a greater man, and those things that were at one time simply dreams, will, in the course of time, become actual realities.

The power of love is another force in this higher group that is extremely valuable, and the reason is that it is the tendency of love to turn attention upon the ideal, the beautiful and the more perfect. When you love somebody, you do not look for their faults; in fact, you do not see their faults. Your whole attention is turned upon their good qualities, and here, let us remember that whatever we continue to see in others, we develop in ourselves. The power of real love always tend's to draw out into expression the finer elements of mind, character and life. For that reason, we should always love, love much, and love the most ideal and the most perfect that we can discover in everybody and in everything that we may meet in life. We have all discovered that when a man really loves an ideal woman, or the woman that constitutes his ideal, he invariably becomes stronger in character, more powerful in personality, and more able in mind. When a woman loves an ideal man, or her ideal, she invariably becomes more attractive. The beautiful in her nature comes forth into full expression and many times the change is so great that we can hardly believe that she is the same woman. The power of love, if genuine, constant and strong, tends to improve everything in human life; and as this power is one of the higher forces in human nature, we readily understand the reason why. We can therefore without further comment, draw our own conclusions as to how we will use this power in the future.

The last of these finer forces that we shall mention, and possibly the strongest, is that of faith; but we must remember if we wish to use this force, that faith does not constitute a belief or any system of beliefs; it is a mental action—an action that goes into the very spirit of those things which we may think of or apply at the time we exercise faith. When you have faith in yourself you place in action a force that goes into the very depth of your being and tends to arouse all the greater powers and finer elements that you may possess. The same is true when you have faith in a certain faculty or in a certain line of action. The power of faith goes into the spirit of things and makes alive, so to speak, the all that is in you. The power of faith also produces perfect concentration. Whenever you have faith along a certain line, you concentrate perfectly along that line, and you cause all the power that is in your mind or system to work for the one thing you are trying to do. It has been discovered that the amount of energy latent in the human system is nothing less than enormous, and as faith tends to arouse all this energy, we realize how important and how powerful is faith.

The effect of faith upon yourself therefore is beneficial in the highest and largest sense, but this is not its only effect. The more faith you have in yourself, the more faith people will have in you. If you have no confidence in yourself you will never inspire confidence in anybody; but if you thoroughly believe in yourself, people will believe in you and in your work. And when people believe in you, you can accomplish ten times as much as when they have no confidence in you whatever.

When a man has tremendous faith in himself, he becomes a live wire, so to speak. It is such a man that becomes a real and vital power wherever he may live or go. It is such a man who leads the race on and on. It is such a man who really does things, and it is people of such a type that we love the best. They invariably inspire others to love the nobler life and to attempt greater things in life, and for this reason their presence is of exceptional value to the progress of the race. To go into details, however, is not necessary. We all know and appreciate the value of faith. We all know that it is one of the highest and one of the greatest forces that man can exercise; we therefore realize how important it becomes to train ourselves to have unbounded faith in everything and in everybody at all times, and under all circumstances.

With All Thy Faults I Love Thee Still

Thus sings the poet, and we call him sentimental; that is, at first thought we do. But upon second thought we change our minds. We then find that faults and defects are always in the minority, and that the larger part of human nature is so wonderful and so beautiful that it needs must inspire admiration and love in everybody. With all their defects there is nothing more interesting than human beings; and the reason is that for every shortcoming in man there are a thousand admirable qualities. The poet, being inspired by the sublime vision of truth, can see this; therefore, what can he do but love? Whenever his eyes are lifted and whenever his thoughts take wings, his soul declares with greater eloquence than ever before, " What a piece of work is man!" Thus every moment renews his admiration, and every thought rekindles the fire of his love.

XX
THE GREATEST POWER IN MAN

I T is the conclusion of modern psychology that the powers and the possibilities inherent in man are practically unbounded. And this conclusion is based upon two great facts. First, that no limit has been found to anything in human nature; and second, that everything in human nature contains a latent capacity for perpetual development.

The discovery of these two facts—and no discovery of greater importance has appeared in any age—gives man a new conception of himself, a conception, which, when applied, will naturally revolutionize the entire field of human activity.

To be able to discern the real significance of this new conception becomes, therefore, the greatest power in man, and should, in consequence, be given the first thought in all efforts that have advancement attainment or achievement in view. The purpose of each individual should be, not simply to cultivate and apply those possibilities that are now in evidence, but also to develop the power to discern and fathom what really exists within him. This power is the greatest power, because it prepares the way for the attainment and expression of all other powers. It is the power that unlocks the door to all power, and must be understood and applied before anything of greater value can be accomplished through human thought or action.

The principal reason why the average person remains weak and incompetent is found in the fact that he makes no effort to fathom and understand the depths of his real being. He may try to use what is in action on the surface, but he is almost entirely unconscious of the fact that enormous powers are in exist ence in the greater depths of his life. These powers are dormant simply because they have not been called into action, and they will continue to lie dormant until man develops his greatest power—the power to discern what really exists within him.

The fundamental cause of failure is found in the belief that what exists on the surface is all there is of man, and the reason why greatness is a rare exception instead of a universal rule can be traced to the same cause. When the mind discovers that its powers are inexhaustible and that its faculties and talents can be developed to any degree imaginable, the fear of failure will entirely disappear. In its stead will come the conviction that man may attain anything or achieve anything. Whatever circumstances may be today, such a mind will know that all can be changed, that the limitations of the person can be made to pass away, and that the greater desires of the heart can be realized.

That mind that can discern what exists in the depths of the real life of man does not simply change its views as to what man may attain and achieve, but actually begins to draw, in a measure, upon those inexhaustible powers within; and begins accordingly to develop and apply those greater possibilities that this deeper discernment has revealed. When man can see through and understand what exists beneath the surface of his life, the expression of his deeper life will begin, because whatever we become conscious of, that we tend to bring forth into tangible expressions, and since the deeper life contains innumerable possibilities as well as enormous power, it is evident that when this deeper life is clearly discerned and completely taken possession of in the consciousness, practically anything may be attained or achieved. The idea that there is more of man than what appears on the surface should be so constantly and so deeply impressed upon the mind that it becomes a positive conviction, and no thoughts should be

125

placed in action unless it is based upon this conviction. To live, think and act in the realization that " there is more of me " should be the constant aim of every individual, and this more will constantly develop, coming forth in greater and greater measure, giving added power and capacity in life to everything that is in action in the human system.

When the average individual fails, he either blames circumstances or comes to the conclusion that he was not equal to the occasion. He therefore easily gives up and tries to be content with the lesser. But if he knew that there was more in him than what he had applied in his undertaking he would not give up. He would know by developing and applying this more, he positively would succeed where he had previously failed. It is therefore evident that when man gives attention to his greater power—the power to discern the more that is in him—he will never give up until he does succeed, and in consequence he invariably will succeed.

That individual who knows his power does not judge according to appearances. He never permits himself to believe that this or that cannot be done. He knows that those things can be done, because he has discovered what really exists within him. He works in the conviction that he must, can and will succeed, because he has the power ; and it is the truth—he does have the power—we all have the power. To live, think and work in the conviction that there is more of you within the real depths of your being, and to know that this more is so immense that no limit to its power can be found, will cause the mind to come into closer and closer touch with this greater power within, and you will consequently get possession of more and more of this power.

The mind that lives in this attitude opens the door of consciousness, so to speak, to everything in human life that has real quality and worth. It places itself in that position where it can respond to the best that exists within itself, and modern psychology has discovered that this best is extraordinary in quality, limitless in power, and contains possibilities that cannot be numbered.

It is the truth that man is a marvellous being—nothing less than marvellous; and the greatest power in man is the power to discern the marvellousness that really does exist within him.

It is the law that we steadily develop and bring forth whatever we think of the most. It is therefore profitable to think constantly of our deeper nature and to try to fathom the limitlessness and the inexhaustibleness of these great and marvellous depths.

In practical life this mode of thinking will have the same effect upon the personal mind as that which is secured in a wire that is not charged when it touches a wire that is charged. The great within is a live wire; when the mind touches the great within, it becomes charged more and more with those same immense powers; and the mind will constantly be in touch with the great within when it lives, thinks and works in the firm conviction that "there is more of me,"—so much more that it cannot be measured.

We can receive from this deeper life only that which we constantly recognize and constantly realize, because consciousness is the door between the outer life and the great within, and we open the door to those things only of which we become conscious.

The principal reason therefore why the average person does not possess greater powers and talents, is because he is not conscious of more; and he is not conscious of more because he has not vitally recognized the great depths of his real life, and has not tried to consciously fathom the possibilities that are latent within him

The average person lives on the surface. He thinks that the surface is all there is of him, and consequently does not place himself in touch with the live wire of his interior and inexhaustible nature. He does not exercise his greatest power—the power to discern what his whole nature actually contains; therefore, he does not unlock the door to any of his other powers.

This being true, we can readily understand why mortals are weak— they are weak simply because they have chosen weakness; but when they begin to choose power and greatness, they will positively become what they have chosen to become.

We all must admit that there is more in man than what is usually expressed in the average person. We may differ as to how much more, but we must agree that the more should be developed, expressed and applied in everybody. It is wrong, both to the individual and to the race, for anyone to remain in the lesser when it is possible to attain the greater. It is right that we all should ascend to the higher, the greater and the better now. And we all can.

THE END